T0086467

A PSYCHEDELIC TRIP INTO THE MYSTERIES OF LIFE

B.G. Webb

authorHOUSE®

AuthorHouse™
1663 Liberty Drive
Bloomington, IN 47403
www.authorhouse.com
Phone: 1 (800) 839-8640

Published by AuthorHouse 06/20/2017

ISBN: 978-1-5246-9710-5 (sc)
ISBN: 978-1-5246-9713-6 (e)

Dedication

To Marie Currie, Albert Einstein, Pearl Buck, Stephen Hawking, Rachel Carson, William Shirer, Carl Jung and all the other doubters of the world.

May your doubting and questioning gain acceptance so that mankind can truly understand the universe and human behavior.

The Mysteries of the Web of Life

Contents

Introduction

In the 19th Century lamplighters went up and down the streets and lit the gas street lamps to help people find their way through the darkness until they reached their destinations.

Well, I am going to do the same thing in this work. I will be the lamplighter showing the readers things that "turn on the light" and give them more insight into the human condition as they go from one street to another.

By the way, I'm also a guru taking you on a psychedelic trip into the unknown. Pretend you are listening to the music of India, the chants and sounds coming from holy men and beautiful women dancing in unison to the rhythms of drums, sitars and tambourines. Instead of drugs to awaken the mind I will use essays, poems, films, photos, music and art to cause the reader to stop and think, to see things in a different way.

So, get ready to discover something hidden in the darkness that you had perhaps never thought about before. So, go from street to street and experience "shocks" to the mind. Watch out for sudden storms, flashes of lightning, rolls of loud thunder and sudden down pours of rain. Don't shy away from what you may consider obscene. The act or actions are often practiced in nature and by other cultures. Try to free yourself from your own prejudices in order to gain new insights.

Don't be frightened. Now, turn the page and go into the darkness to find new insights about life as a result of a sudden shock being triggered by me your beloved guru. I promise that you will find your journey exciting and rewarding.

" OM OM OM"

Doubt St.

Becoming A Real Person

When I was attending college, I took Philosophy and came to know a remarkable human being. His name was Dr. Celms.

We got to know each other because we had similar experiences. He and his family had recently arrived from a refugee camp from Russia in 1948.

In my case I had come to the U.S.A. in 1938 after The Night Of Broken Glass. I had been saved by an underground group from being killed along with my parents and sister.

At the start of the course, Dr. Celms talked about the need to question -- to doubt -- if one was to understand human beings and the universe.

He was really honoring the great sin of doubt. He said, "By your doubts you become a real person."

What makes me a unique individual? It is my constant quality of doubt, of always thinking thru my actions and beliefs and of seeing something in a different light.

I am also unique because I have learned the need to take action to help others. I learned that in 1938 when a group of Catholics and Lutherans worked together to save me and other Jews during the time of Hitler's policy of ethnic cleansing. To only pray about helping someone in trouble isn't enough. Why? Because there is nobody listening. You must with the help of others take peaceful action.

Sometimes a person must have the courage to act alone to confront what he/she feels is evil. Such action must be peaceful in order to preserve the high moral reasons for the purpose of the person's cause.

Doubt

William Shirer Looks For Answers To The Mysteries Of Life

All of his life William Shirer, probably best known for writing <u>The Rise and Fall of the Third Reich</u>, searched for the meaning of life. This effort is especially seen in his last great work entitled, <u>20th Century Journey</u>: <u>A Native's Return 1945-1988</u>. Shirer was about 88 when he wrote the book and he was aware that death was near. Hence, he wanted to review his life and recheck his beliefs.

Born and raised within a Christian (Presbyterian) family in the Middle West, he began questioning his religious beliefs as life took him first to India to report on Mahatma Gandhi and then to Germany to cover Adolf Hitler.

During the second World War he covered the European theater. By the way, he was especially moved by the Holocaust in terms of what it said about the nature of human beings and how it challenged the concept of an all-powerful and just God.

As a result of his life experiences, Shirer began viewing the dogmas of Christianity as irrational fantasies--- indeed, childish speculations and myths. In 20<u>th</u> Century Journey: A Native's Return he tries to answer some of the great mysteries of human existence. Here are the questions that he tries to answer: What is life? For what purpose? How did it originate? Where did we come from? Where are we going? Does death end it all? What is death? Is death the door to eternity or to nothingness?

While he admits that he was never able to find many answers to these questions, he did come to some conclusions about the nature of mankind and the universe. His conclusions were based on empirical evidence, reason and the observations of many respected intellectuals. He was especially impressed with the teachings of Gandhi, the views of many well-known scientists and the writings of Thomas Jefferson, Carl Becker and Arnold Toynbee.

So, by now you are probably itching to find out the conclusions that he did reach. Right? Well, here they are:

1. He agrees with Carl Becker that "man is but a foundling in the cosmos, abandoned by the forces that created him. Unparented, unassisted and undirected by omniscient or benevolent authority, he fends for himself, and with the aid of his own limited intelligence finds his way about in an indifferent universe."

2. He believes that the world is a very savage place. He states: "The longer I lived and the more I observed, the clearer it became to me that man had progressed little beyond his earlier savage state." In fact, he believes that with the advent of nuclear weapons, mankind has a good chance of destroying itself.

3. He agrees with Gandhi that no one religion or philosophy has the truth. He notes that "all societies had a religion, with its god or gods and goddesses." To him religions endeavored to tame mankind's brutal nature and to give solace to believers by offering some hope of a better here-after. He agrees with Gandhi that one must take what is best from all religions.

4. He recognizes that all organized religions provide valuable humanistic services: ceremonies to mark important stages and events in life, educational opportunities for teaching children right from wrong, charity projects for the community, clergy to preach ethical conduct and a social setting for members to give each other TLC.

5. However, he feels that religions become negative factors in human society when they insist that believers accept irrational dogmas. This results in people rejecting reason and becoming intolerant of others. It detracts from the ethical teachings. It causes followers to seek solutions to problems through prayer rather than through a rational seeking of knowledge and effective actions.

6. Like Gandhi he doesn't believe that Jesus was the son of God or the only way for salvation. To him Jesus, like Siddhartha Gautama and other great religious leaders, was a supreme force for good. Shirer, like Gandhi and Jefferson, found Christ's Sermon on the Mount especially powerful in terms of putting into simple language the rules for ethical conduct.

7. He like Arnold Toynbee and others rejects the idea that the Creator (if there is one) is an all-powerful and merciful being. He often wondered how good Christians credit God for all the good in the world and yet don't hold God responsible then for all the bad. To him it simply didn't make sense. And, unlike many, Shirer isn't willing to let the Almighty off the hook or say that we should not question mysteries that are beyond our comprehension.

8. If mankind doesn't blow itself up first, Shirer feels that reason and science will eventually unlock the mysteries of the universe. Yes, the Big Bang theory will be fully understood. Yes, the theory of evolution will be accepted by the skeptics because of overwhelming empirical evidence.

At the end of the book he tells the reader that he is content to die not knowing all the answers. At least he asked questions. He knows that the mysteries will eventually be understood by hard-working scientists. He says that at the end of his life he feels privileged to have lived and survived through one of the most turbulent centuries in mankind's brutal and savage history.

I personally got a lot out of his book. It helped clarify my thoughts about organized religion. I have found it very difficult to accept on the basis of faith many irrational dogmas of Christianity. I refer especially to such things as the virgin birth and the trinity.

I especially have found it difficult to understand a God that seems to need blood sacrifices. As you recall, in the Old Testament Jehovah requires that the faithful sacrifice lambs at the altar. At one point He tells Abraham to slay his son Isaac at the altar. Fortunately for Isaac, Jehovah changes his mind. I remember as a child finding this account scary. Jehovah seemed to a nine-year old to be a very brutal and savage power figure.

In the New Testament we learn that God required the death of Jesus on the cross to redeem mankind. Again, the blessed Heavenly Father needed a blood sacrifice. I recall as an adult feeling squeamish about participating in Communion. I began finding the whole idea of drinking the wine which symbolically represents the blood of Christ repugnant and nauseous. I found myself thinking, "What kind of Heavenly Father is this? Yuk!"

All of Shirer's books are great and I highly recommend them. He writes well. He expresses so many ideas in such a simple and yet descriptive way. All his books are thought provoking but I think you will find 20th Century Journey: A Native's Return 1945-1988 especially a good read.

NOTE

William Shirer believed that the greatest individual of the 20th Century was GANDHI.
Indeed, he felt that Gandhi's ideas would have as much of an impact as those of Jesus.
It is interesting to note that Gandhi defined God as simply TRUTH.

THE SIN OF DOUBT

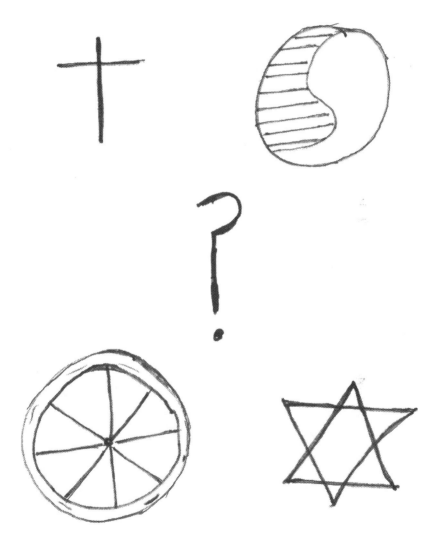

NATURE ST.

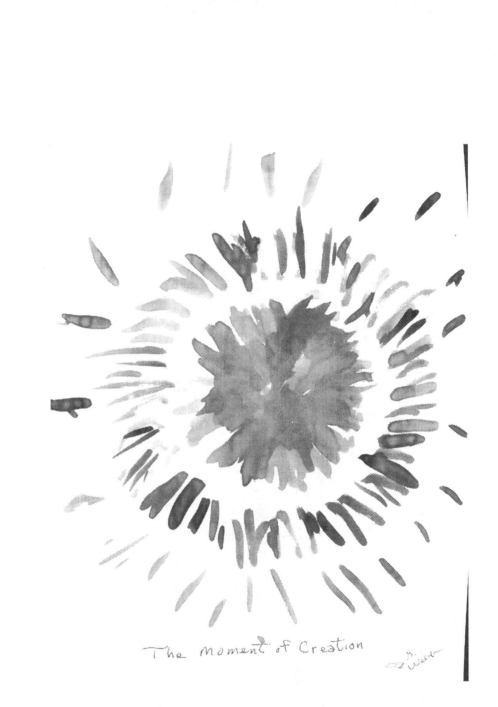

The Moment of Creation

Intelligent Design ?

Am I right in assuming that this intelligence is God or is a one of God's emissaries?

My first question: "Is the essence of I.D. a kind loving God, the same pattern as the Christian God? Am I correct in assuming that this kind God is responsible for the biotic community as it functions? If so let's look at how the biotic community works.

The biotic community is a huge interacting congregation of differing living forms which from geological evidence has probably been in existence for many millions of years. They function from the energy which all they all get from the burning of sugar. Those having the chemical chlorophyll can make the sugar from water and carbon dioxide using the energy from light supplied by the sun. All the other billions of organisms on earth get their energy (food) directly from the plants or from others that eat the plants, and said energy (food) is passed thru many living things. It is easy for most people to understand this food chain as the grasshopper eating the grass, the bird eating the grasshopper, and he hawk eating the bird; but the food chain has many different paths. In addition to the well known paths such as the herbivores, carnivores, and saprophytes there are other more complex and less nice ways of living. Millions of individuals come into existence just to be food for another form of life, and never have a chance to grow up. As example consider the thousands of seeds a plant makes, or the swarms of little fish that hatch. What happens to them; do they all grow up? No, most die sometime during the process, most long before they mature, and in one way another they supply food for others.

Did I.D. create all the millions of parasites just to make other forms of life sick? These parasites and can be large enough for us to see such as ticks and fleas to the ultra small like the viruses. Did I.D. create the virus for HIV so that other parasites could escape the power of the antibodies of their host? (Another thought, perhaps She created the AIDS virus to force man into monogamy; She knew that those who were not monogamous would very likely contact the virus and die.) Aside from the green plants, all other organisms live by the death of many others. Is the all powerful I.D. responsible for establishing such a "crewel" system? If so, we cannot assume that she is a kind merciful God.

Recently someone made the comment that "Yes I know that death is necessary, but I cannot accept the death of small children and especially not babies." I wanted to explain how Mother Nature regulates the number of any organism. People do not like to hear such things, so I held my tongue.

Every organism produces many more young than the ecosystem can accommodate. Any that does not soon become extinct. This rule holds for the plants such as the fern that has millions of spores on the back of its leaves to the animal like the elephant which has a single offspring born after a two year gestation. Thus, children and babies must die otherwise the biotic community would collapse from the over population.

Fellini St.

Fellini Revisited

When I was attending the University of Illinois, I loved going to see a lot of foreign films. At the time they were thought to be daring, provocative and sexy. My favorite directors were Ingmar Bergman, Vittorio and Federico Fellini. I remember all the stimulating discussions that I would have with other foreign film buffs after we had seen one of their works. We would share our thoughts about the characters, the symbolism, the camera work and the themes found in the film. Unlike American directors who centered their attention on entertaining the audience or simply being content to show good and evil, they used innovative film techniques to probe deeply into the human condition and show it in all of its complexity.

Recently, I decided to revisit Fellini to see if I would find his films as stimulating as I did as a student. I went to Blockbusters and rented **La Dolce Vita** which appeared in 1960. After seeing the film again, I can see why I found it so exciting. The film holds up very well in terms of what it has to say about the human condition and in terms of the techniques of creative film making.

The basic story line of **La Dolce Vita** involves a tabloid reporter played by Marcello Mastroianni who sees his life in shallow Rome society as worthless but can't change. The film isn't as complex or as ambiguous as Fellini's brilliant **8 1/2** which has many dreams and flashbacks. Nevertheless, **La Dolce Vita** has most of the characteristics found in all Fellini films.

One thing that Fellini likes to do is to surprise, indeed, shock the viewer. It helps to keep the audience's attention glued to the screen and to hammer home what he is saying about the human condition. He does it at a fast pace. This film opens with a helicopter transporting a large statue. It dangles from a long cable. It is a statue of Jesus. As it is being transported over the city of Rome, large crowds first point at it and then run along its route. Even some sun bathers on top of a roof of a building look up and then wave and shout, "Look! It is Jesus. Hello Jesus!" This is just the beginning of one surprise after another. It also gives the audience a scene of contrast -- the statue of Jesus nearing St. Peter's Cathedral which symbolizes spiritual values-- and the partially naked sun bathers with their voluptuous bodies which symbolize the carnal and sensual aspects of humanity.

As is seen in the opening of the film Fellini is a great one for symbolism. And, the many symbols that he presents in this film provide for foreign film buffs topics for long and interesting discussions. In this film as in all his films, Fellini is making a statement about the meaning of life. In one scene as artists and writers discuss their views one actually sees through an open window search lights moving from one part of the sky to another -- looking and searching. An actor by the name of Frankie has a hairstyle that transforms him into a Satyr. As a creature who is half man, half goat, he is a symbol of Dionysian revelry and decadence as he dances with the buxom American move star named Sylvia who is played by Anita Ekberg. At one point he even walks on his hands and kicks with his legs like a goat. At the end of the film a huge monster fish has been caught in a fishing net. It symbolizes men like Marcello who become ensnared in destructive human behavior. Throughout the film one sees figures with masks of some kind. Often the cabaret dancers have masks. Many of the characters like Marcello wear sun glasses or masks at parties. These "masks" symbolize the desire on the part of some individuals to hide from others and from themselves.

As in all of his films he gives us a slice of life at a very speedy pace. Marcello covers all kinds of news stories in various settings --- from the arrival of an American movie star at an airport to a field where two children claim that they have seen the Madonna to an apartment where two murders and a suicide have taken place. In between covering the these news stories Marcello goes to night clubs and to private parties. Throughout all of these comings and goings Marcello is wrestling with his own confusion about how to love and how to make his life meaningful.

As always there is plenty of contrast in the ilim. You see the very very rich and the very poor. You see the very beautiful and the very grotesque.

You see the concerned intellectual and the shallow, silly, self-indulgent human being. You see those at play and those at prayer. You see the materialistic and the spiritual. And, so typical of a Fellini film you see a wide variety of faces. He was always looking for actors and the so-called "extras" with unusual faces.

He loves to create scenes where the character is the opposite of the setting or locale. In one long series of camera shots he shows Sylvia the buxom American movie star touring of all places the dome of St. Peter's. She is going up a winding staircase to reach one of the look- out points near the top of the dome. She is being followed by reporters like Marcello and the paparazzi. As she makes her rapid ascent, she makes the most ridiculous observations and statements such as "this is great for the diet" and "this should help me lose weight" and "Oh, I'm getting dizzy." At one point she stops and writes her name on the wall. The contrast between the shallow thinking movie star and the religious setting is priceless. Never once does she express any feeling that she is deeply moved spiritually. Her comments are all about herself. She could be touring the Empire State Building.

In all of his films Fellini loves to poke fun at people in general and institutions. This film is particularly hard on the media. It is seen exaggerating and indeed creating news stories. In some cases it is also responsible for causing hysteria among the population. He is also making fun of the public for being so naive. The people are so easily manipulated by the press. In some cases people seem to love being manipulated just so they can be in the newspapers and on TV. Of course, the movie stars are viewed as pathetic human beings who have a love/hate relationship with the press. They need the press to gain and to keep their fame. But they hate the media when it interferes in their personal lives too much.

Fellini also takes a few jabs at the Roman Catholic Church. The whole business of the clergy encouraging and supporting the two children who claim to have seen and spoken to the Madonna makes the Church look ridiculous. Also, in a way, the whole business of a helicopter being used to bring a statue to St. Peter's Cathedral is also a bit much. The Church is seen spending all kinds of money on decorations for the buildings in the Vatican rather than being concerned with more basic spiritual and humans needs -- like helping the poor find food and housing.

Creative camera work enhances the impact of vital scenes in **La Dolce Vita.** By the way the film is done in black and white which in my opinion helps to center the attention of the audience on the emotions of the characters. In one of the early scenes in the film the camera covers the arrival of the movie sex goddess and the her press conference that follows. She is surrounded by reporters and of course the paparazzi. The camera moves in a circle around Sylvia as one question after another is asked. You never see the reporters but only Sylvia at different angles. In a way it is a very amusing sequence because so many of the questions are ridiculous and her answers are too. They ask, "What is your favorite food?" Her response, "Spaghetti." Another asks, "Why are you in films?" Her answer as she heaves and expands her massive bosom, "Because I'm so talented." Then, another reporter asks, "What are the three most important things in your life?" Her response, "Love -- love -- love." The scene is hilarious. And, of course, Sylvia and the paparazzi know it. The whole exchange is a form of play.

Often the camera is filming scenes involving many -- indeed -- hundreds of people. The camera follows the reporters and paparazzi as they are seen running after someone to get a story. The angle of the camera is always surprising. We often find ourselves behind, in front of, in the middle of running crowds. Often we find ourselves high up in a plane or on scaffolding looking down at rushing crowds of people or following cars along a road. In the cabaret scenes the camera moves in on moving breasts and butts as they give motion to the rhythm of the music.

In one sequence we find ourselves among hundreds of "pilgrims" many of whom are in wheelchairs and on crutches who have come to see the children who claim that they have seen and spoken to the Virgin Mary. In one scene the two children keep everyone rushing about by saying, "The Madonna is over there" -- then pointing and saying, "Now she is over there." Then, in a remarkable scene it starts to rain and the "pilgrims" are seen rushing from one area to another. Some of the huge search lights that are illuminating the area blow up because of the rain. This does stop the faithful -- some of whom carry their sick relatives on stretchers -- as they search for the Virgin Mary who they believe has the power to heal. Finally, the children announce, "The Madonna has told us that a church should be built here." The final scenes show the people ripping apart the tree under which the Virgin Mary had supposedly first appeared. They view it as a sacred relic and believe that even one of its small leaves might contain mystical power. Unfortunately, in the frenzy one poor "pilgrim" has been trampled to death -- his body lies on the wet ground. A priest appears -- kneels by the man and gives him last rites.

Lights and shadows are used effectively throughout the film. Again, this shows Fellini's skill in using black and white film which lends itself to using lights and shadows to enhance the interpretation of a character as well as the surrounding atmosphere. People are seen using candles and flash lights to await the children and perhaps see the reappearance of the Madonna. People are seen using torches to go through an old castle at one of the off-beat parties that Marcello attends. When Sylvia wanders through some of the streets of Rome looking for a lost kitten which perhaps symbolizes her lost childlike innocence, lights and shadows are used every effectively.

In all Fellini films there is a serious quest to find some truth about the human condition. Indeed, the title of the film, **La Dolce Vita** which translates as "the sweet or good life" gives us a clue with regard to Fellini's overall purpose. He is asking, "What is the good life?" All the excesses, camera work, surprises are designed to achieve the director's serious purpose. In this case the main character Marcello is given chances to turn away from his worthless life as a reporter for cheap tabloids but refuses. He has become too ensnared in his worthless life and destructive behavior. In a larger way, I think that Fellini is saying to all of us to make correct choices so that our lives can have some value. That is what he is doing by making films that are not just entertaining but saying something about the human condition. This idea of taking action in a worthwhile endeavor goes along with the philosophy of atheistic Existentialism which Fellini had embraced. He believed that since there isn't a God or definite moral standards in our meaningless universe that we must take charge -- make decisions that give our lives meaning -- which provide happiness for ourselves and others. We do these worthwhile things not for some reward in an nonexistent afterlife or to please some deity or because we fear eternal punishment from an angry god but because we want to be true to our own values that give our lives meaning and happiness. In so doing, we prove that we exist -- that we have an impact even though it may be in a very small way.

Also, another theme is about Marcello's problem with love -- truly being able to commit himself to one individual in a mature loving way. Unfortunately, he never learns to do this. Instead, we find him being temporarily infatuated with one woman after another. We meet his father in the film and discover that his father -- a traveling champagne salesman -- has the same problem. But, Marcello seems unable to break the pattern and instead seems to be destined to repeat it again and again. We realize that he will never be able to really love one woman or as far as that goes one human being. Love to him means simply sexual passion or an infatuation and not an unselfish commitment to another human being. This theme of the importance of learning how to love was a deep concern to Fellini and it is found in many of his other films -- especially **8 1/2**. He probably had a lot of problems with this in his own life.

Another theme of the film is more disturbing. In the film a creative artist by the name of Steiner seemingly has made the right choices -- he has a good marriage -- he has a lovely family -- he is making a positive contribution in terms of his writing career -- and he seems to have made peace with the Roman Catholic Church. He even tries to help Marcello by offering him opportunities to be a serious writer. Then, Fellini throws us a curve -- Steiner murders his two young children and commits suicide. I'm sure that most viewers like myself asked, "What is going on here?" Then, we remember a conversation that Steiner had with Marcello in which he says that in order to achieve complete happiness that one must be suspended in a happy period of life. He tells Marcello that he is especially happy when he is close to his children. He talks about how wonderful he feels when his two children come and sleep with him in the same bed. He feels that their mutual love for each other gives them great happiness. So, are we to assume that Steiner decided to do what he did so that he and his two children could be in that happy situation for eternity? I guess so. Fellini probably felt that one should choose when to die -- and to do it when one is supremely happy. This idea was probably an extension of his belief in Existentialism.

Another aspect of the film that I did not recognize when I first saw it but now I do is that this film -- and so many of his others -- are surrealistic.

I have been reading a lot lately about the art movement called surrealism and especially the life and works of Salvador Dali. I think that Fellini was making an attempt in various parts of the film to create surrealism on film -- creating fantastic imagery through often unnatural combinations.

Well, my revisit to Fellini certainly was worthwhile -- very thought provoking. And, that is a tribute to Fellini. He wanted to make a statement about the human condition and to jolt the viewer into thinking about profound questions of life and existence. Even after all these years **La Dolce Vita** packs a wallop. In my opinion the film is still current. We are still wrestling with the same questions brought up in the film.

Religion St.

Looking Though The Glass Darkly

Get ready for something close and personal. My title reflects how I have felt most of my life.

Of course, the idea embodied in the phrase comes from Corinthians I, chapter 13, verse 12. Here it is: "For now we see through a glass darkly, but then face to face; now I know in part; but then shall I know even as also I am known."

I can't remember when verse 12 took on a more important meaning for me. I think that it was after seeing the movie *Wild Strawberries* which was directed by Igmar Bergmann In that movie, as a distinguished professor travels to receive a national award, he reviews his life. Despite enjoying professional success, he must face the fact that he had failed to understand the relationships around him and life in general. During the film verse 12 is often read or spoken by the characters.

It took me a long time to realize that I was in the dark. As a child I thought that I knew the truth. I accepted without question the Christian doctrines about the universe, the nature of man and my relationship to others. I did this despite having relatives -- especially on my mother's side -- who were members of other faiths or none whatsoever. I was told by my parents that they were wrong.

Even as a college sophomore I assumed that I understood the world around me. Then things began to challenge my clear image of the world.

The glass I was looking through suddenly got darker.

During my junior year I was required by take Introduction to Philosophy. There I was introduced to other ways of looking at life. I remember being especially impressed with the Greeks and some of the modern "isms" such as existentialism. I was made aware of mass culture and how it was shaped by the dominant groups in society and more importantly how it gives a distorted view of the world. The course challenged my preconceived ideas. I began to realize that I was in the dark -- that I was looking through a glass darkly.

During my senior year I was required to enroll in Religions of the World where I studied in depth the other great religious systems. I remember being especially fascinated with Hinduism and the idea that there are many paths to the same goal. Well, I suddenly found myself doubting my faith in Christianity and its teachings about the world around me. I am sure that the professors at Augustana College didn't mean that to- happen but it did. Along with my doubts came an-increasing lack of understanding of the world around me. Things that-had appeared to-be so simple -- so clearly defined -- were suddenly behind a dark and foggy glass.

Later, as I experienced life and met more people with different views about humankind, I became even more uncertain. I especially remember meeting a graduate student at the University of Illinois by the name of Henry Lowenthau who was an atheist. He was getting his M.A. in anthropology and of course had very different ideas about things. He was always viewing life in terms of nature and what science had discovered about it. After sharing ideas with Henry, I saw the glass getting darker and darker.

When I reread chapter 13 of I Corinthians, I found verse 11 very appropriate to my situation. It reads: "When I was a child, I spake as a child, I understood as a child, I thought as a child; but when I became a man, I put away childish things." I began to realize that many of the doctrines and ideas that I had embraced without question were part of "childish things."

Over the years I found that working with people from different academic areas broadened and deepened my outlook. When I was teaching at Webster Groves High School, I team taught with teachers from different disciples. One of them was a woman by the name of Wilda Swift who had majored in sociology and anthropology. Together we created a unit entitled, "What is a human being?" It assigned the students to read **The Human Ape** and **The Human Zoo.** Both books gave me and the students a different view of human nature because it was from a naturalist's point of view. I found that the darkness that surrounded me was lifted somewhat by looking at humans from a purely anthropological view rather and a religious one. Of course, along with it came a feeling of uneasiness as I gave up my traditional beliefs. The uneasiness verified in my mind how powerful a hold the dominant groups can have on individuals in a society as well as how difficult it is to truly enjoy freedom of thought in any society.

Having the time in retirement to read about and ponder the mysteries of life has been very beneficial. Albert Einstein's writings have been illuminating. I remember that he declared, "You can understand things better if you look at the nature of things in the world." I also found Pearl Buck's thoughts very helpful. She felt that both the scientist and the religionist were both peering through the darken glass --- each trying to come up with the truth. She believed that mysteries are "simply questions that haven't been answered yet -- and that the scientists would discover the natural solutions to them all eventually." She was content to leave it at that. Unlike so many humans she didn't feel the need to decide on solutions or final answers. I guess she placed her faith in science and if there is one, an understanding Deity.

Another book that I found very revealing was William Shirer's A **Native's Return.** In it he talked about how his Presbyterian faith gave way to skepticism as he traveled throughout the world and was exposed to many religions and religious leaders like Gandhi. He was especially troubled by how a good God could allow so much evil and suffering.

For me, life continues to be in the twilight. I am not able to see myself, others and world around me clearly. I look through the glass darkly.

A Requirement For Human Evolution—Religion

I am not going to prove or even suggest that any religion is factually true, nor am I going to condemn religion because it is contrary to empirical fact. Religions are all based on improbable myths and, contrary to an often-heard statement, they are not at all compatible with each other. What I am proposing is that the development of religion was essential human evolution. To put my very shocking theory succinct, it was religion, in conjunction with a series of cellular mutations that changed the man-like apes into Homo sapiens.

For several years I have been impressed by a very interesting fact and I have repeatedly proposed this idea whenever I have a chance. Most people agree with me but attach no significance to it. I have never heard or read any biologist commenting on the very obvious fact. My observation "All human cultures have a religion." indicates to me that this is not just coincidental but it is an essential factor of humanity. It is not only essential but may well be part of the engine that produced modern man.

In what way is it essential? Most religions give some kind of an explanation of how the whole earth, animals and man came into being and propose some kind of ruler of the universe, a god. This god by way of myths and stories tells the people how to behave, what to do and what not to do. Probably the stories also helped create the ceremonies that molded groups of individuals into functioning units and was the kernel around which great art was generated. I am proposing that this behavior control and production of interacting groups and generation of art might well be important factors in making us human.

It is very interesting that complex social society has evolved only three times, twice in two very different Orders of insects, the Hymenoptera (bees, ants and wasps) and the Isoptera (Termites) and in just one Vertebrate, man. We are the only Mammal with a complex social structure; true many others such as dogs, wolves, monkeys and apes live in social groups but without the degree of complexity seen in human societies. The social structure of the bees, ants, wasps and termites is very different from ours. Socialization demands a differentiation of rolls and some force to regulate behavior. A great difference between the two kinds of socialization is how behavior is controlled and how the rolls are differentiated. For the insects their behavior seems to be hard wired and very little if any dependent on learning. Our behavior is controlled by learning and rules enforced by social pressure.

The difference between inborn behavior and learned patterns is undoubtedly a result of physiologic difference in the body, in the brain, nerves, hormones etc. During the million or so years that pre-humans learned to walk upright and use the hands to effectively manipulate tools, conceptual thought and language developed. Now they were ready for even greater changes. I am proposing this idea in a very simplified and shortened manner. The new brain started to ask questions of where, how, and why and to answer these questions by creating stories: the myths that became the basis for the religions, and these religions promulgated rules that social pressure enforced. Thus the early developing religion was one of the factors that nudged modern man into existence.

The higher apes from which we evolved had simple social groups that were usually controlled by the Alpha individual, but such control could at best be only crude and could not regulate the infinite variations necessary in human society. As the brains of the apes developed, changes gradually came into play, any group with a religion with an overlaying umbrella of social concepts (values) could facilitated finer control, and the society would prosper. This is the engine of evolution. If it works, the group prospers, and usually the new factor becomes progressively more effective. The uniqueness of my proposal is that it is not a biologic change but rather a change in social structure that makes the difference.

Has religion created undesirable actions? Yes, without a doubt. We Agnostic/humanistic types can easily point out how it has repeatedly stifled intellectual thought in the past and still does. It has created terrible destructive wars, persecution, hatred and on on. We can look to other world religions and back to the development of our own Judeo-Christian faiths and see many examples of great cruelty and persecution. Evolution also produces some pretty weird forms; look at the ridiculous horns, beaks, feathers, etc on many animals. They may be a hindrance, and even fatal to some individuals, but if it furthers reproductive success, it will be favored. Evolution only sees the overall success, not what happens to the individual.

This flight into individual thought has given me an answer to a very troubling question. There is one Christian denomination that, to me, has ridiculous basic tenets but has created a wonderful sub culture of our society. I am speaking of the Christian Scientists. Those that I now know are in general very intelligent, well-educated and upper middle class and are in general wonderful people. They have modified their anti medicine stance greatly from that of the friends that I knew as a child. Now in practice, if not officially sanctioned by the mother church, they have modify the faith so that they do use modern medicine. The Christian Scientist Monitor is a first rate newspaper, with only one daily article that is about their faith. Yesterday I forced myself to read this religion article and in it I saw some of the same change in outlook that I have seen in the people I know. They admit the validity of modern medicine, but also give some room for faith healing. In all other articles that might bear on religion are covered in a complete even-handed manner. Is it possible that, as 1 am beginning to conclude, the worth of a religion is more accurately based on the quality of culture it produces than on the validity of its myths.

In many respects I am shocked at what I am saying: "A religion is good, and is a benefit without regard to its consistency with empirical fact." But look at these empirical facts:

1. All cultures have a religion
2. Religion is a much more effective engine of behavior control than any dictator, and no set of laws can be detailed enough to cover all aspects of our lives.
3. Religion is the basis of much if not most of the great art: Music, dance, sculpture, painting and even architecture
4. Whatever its theology, all religions form cohesive groups of interacting individuals.

Where does this leave those like me, those who insist that my religion be consistent with empirical fact? Out of step? You bet! I can not deny my own intellect, which I consider the most defining part of me, to the dictate of any religion. I can easily see that religion is not my only spot of rebellion. I make most decisions on an intellectual basis. However human culture could not come into being with too many like me, nor would it have advanced nearly as far without a few free thinkers.

Unusual St.

Four Unusual College Roommates

As a college student at the University of Illinois I had to adjust to living with a lot of roommates in the dorms. The follow are descriptions of four of the most interesting "characters" that I lived with.

#1 Jim - He had a fatal obsession.

Jim was 5'4" with a small frame. While he was brilliant in physics, he had difficulty communicating with people. He often stuttered when he became too excited. With his baby face, thick glasses and crew cut he personified the term "nerd."

When I talked with him, he always came across as a sincere and sensitive guy. The thing that made him unforgettable was that he became utterly obsessed with meeting and dating Nancy Fleming -- who was Miss America of 1961.

Jim had watched her selection and crowning on TV and had become very attracted to her. He started writing letters to her and telling everyone that he thought that "she was the most beautiful girl in the world." He received a form letter back from the Miss America Pageant organization with a black and white publicity photo of Miss America. I remember that it was even signed, "Affectionally, Nancy Fleming." Jim immediately had it framed and placed on his desk.

Jim's obsession stopped there until one day he read in the local newspaper that Miss America would be coming to visit the Champaign-Urbana area. This resulted in Jim becoming ecstatic about the prospect of actually being able to see and meet Nancy Fleming in person. I told him, "Jim, she won't remember getting a letter from you." Of course, Jim didn't believe me. He called the Chamber of Commerce to find out about the details of her visit. He was told about her itinerary: the arrival time at the airport, the meeting with the mayor at City Hall, and the welcoming parade to honor her. Jim was even told that she would be staying at the Lincoln Hotel in Urbana.

The day Miss America arrived, Jim and I were at the airport to see her plane land. Jim waved wildly to her as she got off the plane and spoke to reporters. Then, we drove back to Champaign to see the ceremonies at City Hall and the parade that followed. Again, Jim waved enthusiastically at her as she passed us by on a specially built float. Of course, she waved back and smiled at us along with every other person standing on the curb. However, Jim took this personally and whispered to me, "See Bud, she knows who I am."

Later that night Jim tried to visit her at the Lincoln Hotel. I was sitting in the room when he called the hotel and asked to speak with her. Her private secretary refused to let his call go through. At that point, I exclaimed, "Jim, you're making a fool of yourself. She is not going to see you." Later, he went to the hotel. After he returned, he told me that he had stood in the lobby and later outside the entrance hoping to get a glimpse of Miss America.

The next day Jim read in the newspaper that Miss America had come down with the flu and had been moved to a hospital in Urbana. Well, Jim immediately went to the hospital and tried to gain access to her room. Naturally, he was arrested by the police and charged with disturbing the peace.

I didn't see Jim until much later. His father had to fly in from New Jersey to bail him out. At the hearing Jim was fined and placed on probation. He had to agree to go into counseling. I guess he gradually worked out his problems. He never did tell me anything about his therapy sessions.

Jim eventually met a girl at the Presbyterian Church which was located a few blocks from campus. As I recall they both sang in the choir. Well, they were married after he received his Ph.D. in Physics and then moved to the Chicago area where Jim started teaching at the Illinois Institute of Technology.

I have often wondered if Jim ever had another fatal attraction incident. For years after that any news story about some crazy fan made me wonder, "Is it Jim?" To this day I still wonder if a person can truly be cured of having fatal attractions. Jim's case was particularly disturbing to me because I knew him and he seemed like such an intelligent and nice guy.

#2 Vince - He believed that all sinners needed to be punished -- and harshly too.

While Vince was only about 5'8", he possessed a lot of animal magnetism due to his square jaw, prominent nose, strong white teeth and steel blue eyes. His complexion was marred with scars left from a bad bout with the smallpox. He had a rather pleasant smile when things were going his way. However, he also could be very cross and fierce looking when he disapproved of something. On those occasions when he became enraged about something, his face took on the appearance of a snarling wolf.

He was from the Chicago area and was very proud of his Italian heritage. He felt that Italians were portrayed badly on TV and in films. He railed against the implication that all Italians were part of the Mafia.

Vince was the only boy in his family. He had three sisters -- Rosa, Maria and Margarita -- who seemed to adore him. I got the impression that he was the favorite child and that his sisters always had to take a back seat to him.

He went to West Point as a freshman but had to drop out because of his low grades. However, he still wore with pride his brown bathrobe from West Point. He told me that the things he liked the most about West Point were "the strict rules" and "the chain of command."

As a roommate he immediately told me that we had to have rules and regulations. He suggested setting down rules pertaining to the following: when we should have quiet study time, who should clean the room and bathroom and on what days, and who could be allowed in our room and when. While I went along with him, after awhile I felt that I was his captive -- that the rules were designed to control me. I began to recognize that Vince was a control freak.

Vince was also into excessive neatness and cleanliness. Everything had to be kept in order. He became very upset if something or someone changed the room in any way. Once, he accused me of removing one is his pens from his desk. As I looked into his angry eyes, I thought to myself, "My God, it's Mr. Hyde!"

He took great pride in his appearance. He could be a snob when it came to the quality of one's clothes. He sometimes showed me the labels on his shirts and ties to indicate that they were of quality. He told me that he always purchased his suits, shirts, ties and shoes from Brooks Brothers in Chicago. His prize possession was a brown overcoat made of camel hair. Naturally, he always wore his London Fog trench coat when it rained.

He often spoke about what he called the "rough life" being the best for a person's character. He believed that a little pain was good for the soul. I noticed that he never wore a cap or hat of any kind even on very cold days. Despite rain and snow Vince would always be hatless. Of course, he would never be caught dead using an umbrella. I never understood how he stood the cold. His ears and nose would turn red from the biting wind. I guess his desire to project a macho image overcame his feelings of discomfort.

In my case I found that I had to be well covered to deal with the harsh cold winds and downpours that swept out of the surrounding prairie and into the campus of the University of Illinois. Yes, I was one of those those guys who wore caps and scarfs and carried an umbrella. Naturally, Vince denounced me as a mama's boy who was too delicate for the rough life of a real man. Once he told me, "Bud, I will not walk with you if you insist on wearing that fur hat and especially that wool scarf around your face." Of course, I refused. I told him that I wasn't going to "freeze my ass off" to please him. So, that day Vince who by this time I was secretly calling "Mr. Hyde" walked by himself.

Vince was a devout Roman Catholic. He went to Mass daily and frequently took advantage of the Confessional to cleanse his soul. He felt that most Catholics on campus were not disciplined enough-- not really true to their faith. He really liked Father Duncan who was the priest at the Newman Center. The latter was known for his fire and brimstone sermons and his hash judgmental statements. Once, looking at students coming up to the railing to receive the eucharistic bread, he said, "Yes, you stick out your tongues like fish to receive the Body of Christ -- and then you go out and commit unspeakable carnal sins." While some students were offended by such remarks, Vince thought they were great. He would tell me, "Yeah, Father Duncan sure gave them hell -- and they deserved it too -- the fornicators!" Father Duncan often went to stand in the lobby of the

U. of I. movie theatre to catch Catholic students who were seeing movies that had been banned by the Church. Vince applauded this effort too.

Vince and I finally came to the parting of the ways when he caught me necking with my girl friend in our room. I had thought that he would be staying in Chicago for an extra day, so I had invited Jill to the room to enjoy some private time together. We were certainly surprised to find Vince unlocking the door and interrupting our tete-a-tete. Well, you would have thought that Vince was John the Baptist or John Calvin or Billy Sunday (I'm trying to be ecumenical.) who had discovered someone committing an unpardonable sin. He denounced us both and then stormed out of the room. He immediately signed up for another room for the next semester. I guess he felt that he couldn't possibly co-exist with a carnal guy like me. Frankly, I was relieved. Living with the wolfish Mr. Hyde was getting to me.

By the way, my next "roomy" was Elliot who urged me to join him during the summer to work at the Boom Boom Club on Rush Street in Chicago. Boy, talk about a change of perspective and temperament. Just what I needed.

I learned later that Vince became a teacher in one of the better Catholic schools in the Chicago area. He never married which was probably for the best. Over the years I often found myself saying a silent prayer for his students.

#3 Benjamin - He only dated girls who were members of the Junior League.

Benjamin or Benny as we called him was from New England -- Newton, Massachusetts to be exact. He had graduated from Harvard and then had decided to go west to get an M.A. in political science at the University of Illinois. He was a strange looking guy -- short, plump, rabbity looking. His basically shy quiet nature along with his large pleading hazel eyes that looked out at you through thick-lensed, horn rimmed glasses made him seem all the more like a timid rabbit.

While he wore jackets and bow ties, he always looked unkempt. His hair was never combed and he did not shave daily. He was also a chain smoker and often you could see ashes on his clothes along with holes that the hot ashes had burned into his pants, ties and jackets.

The smell of whiskey was often on his breath. He kept a bottle of Scotch whiskey in his bottom dresser drawer and took a nip now and then. He usually went on a drinking bender after completing a major research project. Once I found him lying on the floor in the middle of our room so drunk that his skin felt cold and clammy like wet clay. When his eyes finally focused on me as I bent over him, he slurred, "Bu--Bu-- Bud! You-- you're the best roommmm--ate that I ev--ever had." Then, he told me that he felt sick to his stomach. I immediately recruited five guys from our floor to help me carry him to the bathroom so he could throw up in the toilet. After that I gave him some baking soda in warm water to settle his "inners" and then helped him into bed.

I enjoyed talking to Benny because he was so knowledgeable about so many things. I found that it is true that Harvard graduates are quite intelligent. Of course, in Benny's case he was not only bright but eccentric -- and a drunk.

Once in awhile he would date a girl on campus but he had one strict requirement -- she had to be a member of the Junior League. I guess he felt that membership in that organization ensured her commitment to social action and proof that she came from a progressive and respectable family. By the way, I had never heard of the Junior League until I met rabbity Benny.

Benny was an early supporter of John F. Kennedy. In fact, Benny was one of the leaders of the Kennedy for President movement on campus. The group met at one of the watering holes (the Turk's Head I think) off campus. I started going to meetings with Benny and decided that this guy Kennedy might be a good candidate. Since Adlai Stevenson had run two times already, I thought someone new had a better chance of defeating Richard Nixon.

It was at one of these meetings that Benny met Wilma, a graduate student in the English. Of course, she was a member of the Junior League. Also, like Benny she was short, plump and rabbity looking. They quickly became immersed in each other. They seemed to be a funny and strange twosome to a lot of us. In their case love became a passionate frenzy. That's the only way I can describe it. They often could be seen sharing the same coat as they walked or more likely ran like two frightened rabbits across campus. This allowed them to be as close to each other as possible. Even when they ate at the Student Union and stood in the serving line, the two were so interwoven that they could have been mistaken for Siamese twins.

By the way they were ideal drinking buddies. When they went to a bar together, Wilma often sat on Benny's lap and shared the same stool -- and the same drink. Sober or tipsey they were a cute couple. They would coo and ah and goo goo with one another as they enjoyed those funny silly words and sounds that lovers share. Usually, at a certain point in their tete-a-tete Wilma would start giggling -- followed by Benny as they tickled each other. Everyone in the tavern would look in their direction and simply smile. They were so lovable. Frankly, Wilma had a positive effect on Benny's drinking. Now, he didn't drink to forget but to celebrate the love in his life. He became a happy drunk.

One day they rushed into the dorm room and seemed ready to make passionate love before my very eyes. I quietly excused myself so they could go at it. Later, Benny and I worked out an arrangement so that he and Wilma could have the room at certain times. I didn't mind as long as I could be back in the room by 10:00 p.m. Who was I to deny such passionate young love?

As the secretary of the Kennedy For President Committee, Benny sent letters to Senator John F. Kennedy and Mrs. Eleanor Roosevelt inviting them to speak on campus. Much to our surprise, both accepted the invitations. So, Benny and the rest of us on the committee had a lot of work to do. We got permission from the University for the speakers to appear at certain places and we also advertised the up-coming events on the local TV and radio stations.

Mrs. Roosevelt was scheduled to appear at the small auditorium in Lincoln Hall while Kennedy was booked to appear in the quadrangle. As I recall both spoke around the lunch hour on different days. Kennedy drew a large enthusiastic crowd in the thousands while Mrs. Roosevelt spoke to only about two hundred students. Kennedy's appearance was unforgettable. He was like a Greek god -- a tall, handsome, virile man with a radiant smile and a gorgeous suntan.

Benny was the one who had the responsibility to greet Mrs. Roosevelt and later introduce her to the audience. I wondered how she would respond to him. Of course, on that day he really made an effort to clean himself up. He had actually combed his hair and shaved. I only noticed one cigarette hole and smelled a touch of whiskey which he had cleverly tried to hide by using a lot of Old Spice aftershave.

Much to my surprise and relief Mrs. Roosevelt took him in stride. She kept smiling as she graciously shook his hand and chatted with him before he introduced her. Ben later told me that he discovered that he had to speak loudly to Mrs. Roosevelt because she was very hard of hearing despite the fact that she wore glass frames with hearing aids in them.

After Benny received his M.A., he and Wilma were married and moved to Iowa City where he worked on his Ph.D. The last I heard the couple had a little girl and Benny was teaching in a college on the east coast. I guess he was right about only dating a girl who was a member of the Junior League because the two seemed to be a perfect match.

#4 Nazir - He was corrupted by American culture -- at least I think he was.

One of the most memorable surprises in my life occurred when I opened the door to my assigned room in the new grad dorm and looked into the dark handsome face of Nazir. I have to admit I was apprehensive about the situation at first. Like a lot of whites I had never lived on a daily basis with someone of a different skin color and from a totally different culture.

I quickly found out that Nazir was a graduate student in business management who had been born in Benares, India. He was short (about 5'6"), muscular with a thick head of black hair and a mustache. He had very large and expressive black eyes. His pleasing sounding baritone voice along with his warm smile and outgoing personality added to his magnetism.

He kept in shape by playing soccer as often as he could. When I would see him playing on the field, he reminded me of a beautiful black Arabian horse -- so dexterous -- so filled with physical energy.

When I first met him he was very religious. He had been brought up as a strict Moslem. He insisted on praying five times a day facing Mecca. He religiously read the **Koran** and spoke often of the teachings of Muhammed -- especially the idea that we are all brothers. He religiously avoided eating pork, drinking alcoholic beverages and smoking in accordance with the strict rules of his faith.

I started going with him to various gatherings of the Indian community on campus. Nazir and his Indian friends represented to me an exotic and romantic culture. I found myself enjoying the spicy foods, the rhythmic music, the colorful saris and turbans, and the discussions about Hindu gods and goddesses as well as the future of India. I also found myself really liking Nazir; he seemed so earnest and sincere -- a man of principle.

As he began to experience American life, Nazir changed. At first he only dated Indian girls on campus but one day he told me that he found them to be "too passive." He wanted to have sex with them and they refused. One of his close Indian friends was dating a beautiful blond American girl who "put out." Having a blond girl friend gave the man lots of status. Suddenly, Nazir became obsessed with the idea of dating a blond American girl. He finally met a girl by the name of Sherry who was very happy to go out with him. She was a shy, quiet girl who was very tall -- about 6'2". She seemed to be very sensitive and vulnerable. Nazir convinced her to dye her hair blond. He confided to me that she also dyed her pubic hair which he found a real "turn on." So, he got his wish. Sherry became his trophy -- his status symbol. She appeared to be very much in love with him. Once I asked him if he felt uneasy about her height and he replied, "No Bud, I enjoy the climb." By that time they were having sex on a regular basis. By the way, he did not like condoms. He solved "his problem" by getting some birth control pills (which were illegal in this country at the time) for Sherry to take. At the time, I remember being concerned about Sherry. I liked her a lot and felt that she was being used by Nazir as a sex toy.

Nazir was also becoming more materialistic. He wanted money so that he could get an apartment and have a car. He was able to get several jobs and to save enough to buy a nice used car to drive Sherry around town. Eventually, he moved out of the dorm and rented a "love nest" for himself and his blonde.

His new philosophy reflected his new found materialism. He told me that in order to get ahead, one had to be a hustler -- and often a dishonest one at that. He started smoking cigars and drinking rum and vodka now and then. He told me that he had learned that a person had to bend one's personal beliefs to go along with the business scene. He declared, "It's important to be in the with the right people so you can use them to get ahead."

He also was becoming less sensitive to his fellowman. I remember asking him about his concern for the poor of India. It was during our Thanksgiving season and I explained, "Nazir, we often give food to those who are less fortunate than ourselves during this season." He looked at me and declared, "Oh, don't worry about the poor of India. There has always been plenty of poor people there for centuries. I have learned to go out and enjoy myself and not worry about any of them."

Nazir also did nothing to defend African Americans in this country. When he went to a barber shop off campus, the owner of the shop at first refused to cut his hair because he thought that Nazir was a Negro. Well, Nazir set him straight. He told the man that he was an Aryan Indian -- and "not one of your filthy American niggers." So much for the Moslem concept of brotherhood.

Eventually, Nazir received his Ph.D. in Business Management, dumped his bogus blonde, returned to India to marry an Indian girl (a virgin) who had been selected by his parents, and took a job with an international corporation. He did quite well. He had a home in India, England, and an apartment in Miami. When he called me to talk about his success, he added that he had a mistress -- this time a real blonde. So, Nazir certainly attained the great American dream. Unfortunately, in some ways he absorbed the worst elements of so-called American culture. The Nazir that I first met and really liked was nowhere to be found.

Of course, I could be wrong. Perhaps I have been too hard on American culture. It is possible that the real Nazir -- the materialist opportunist -- the licentious user of women was always there. He was hiding behind a facade of religious devotion for the Islamic faith. His ethical system rested on quicksand. The freedom of American culture simply gave him the opportunity to "come out of the closet" sort of speak -- make the choices that reflected his real value system. That would explain why he changed so rapidly and with such great enthusiasm. Could be.

Murder St.

Murder In The Dorm

My title for this piece sounds like a title of a murder mystery written by Agatha Christie. Unfortunately, in this case everything I'm going to tell you is the truth.

I had a hard time deciding how I should tell you about the murder that I witnessed. I finally decided to relate certain incidents that led up to the murder -- then to describe the horrible murder itself -- and finally tell you what I found out later about the murderer and his victim from the TV news and local newspapers.

The murder happened in Urbana, Illinois at the Graduate Dorm on Green Street in March of 1962.

So, let's start with the incidents -- really encounters -- that I witnessed before the brutal crime. Let me be clear about something. I never knew exactly what was going on when I observed these incidents. I certainly did not believe that they would result in murder.

September, 1961

I met several friends for lunch at the cafeteria in the Home Economics Building. While I was eating I looked over at the next table and saw a man who must have been in his early 40s eating with a young woman in her 20's. They seemed to be enjoying their time together. The man was the classic tall, dark and handsome type. He seemed to be very outgoing -- seemed to love to talk and to laugh. The young lady was petite with long blond hair and a slim figure. She seemed to be listening intently to what the man was saying. As he gestured with his right arm, he moved his jacket upward long enough for me to see that he was carrying a gun in a holster.

October and November, 1961

Several times as I walked along the quadrangle from Lincoln Hall to the Student Union I saw the same couple walking hand in hand -- obviously very much in love. As the weather got colder, the man started wearing a long, heavy black overcoat which made him seem out of place since most of the students simply wore short winter jackets.

January, 1962

As I was eating in the main dining room at the Student Union, I noticed the blond young woman eating with several other students. I wondered, "Where is tall, dark and handsome?" Then I saw him -- he was standing in the hall outside the cafeteria near one of the staircases. He had his long black overcoat on and an intense look of anxiety on his face. As the blonde and her friends came near him, he yelled, "Jennifer, I want to talk to you." The blonde stayed close to her friends as she replied, "Todd, there is nothing to talk about." As she ran up the stairs, the man in the overcoat yelled," But, it will only take a few minutes."

February, 1962

As I was looking out the window of my room in the dorm, I saw a car filled with several people pull up into the parking lot. Jennifer stepped out of the car and started walking toward the front entrance. Then, I saw a man step out of another car -- it was Todd. As he started running after Jennifer, she turned and recognized him. She said something to him (I was unable to hear what she said) as he tried to take hold of her shoulders. Then, two people got out of the car in which Jennifer had been in. I think that they yelled, "Leave her alone." With that Todd stopped what he was doing and Jennifer ran to the front door, opened it and disappeared inside.

March, 1962

I remember it was a Saturday and I had worked all day at the library on a research paper. I decided after eating at the Student Union to go to the commons in the dorm and watch some TV to relax my mind. I found that about ten other students had the same idea. Some were sitting in comfortable chairs while others were sitting on the two sofas that faced the large TV. "Gun smoke" was just starting as I got comfortable in one of the nicer chairs. It was about twenty minutes into the program when we heard the sound of the front door opening and closing behind us. Then we saw Jennifer running past us and around the corner where the door that led to the staircase was located. Todd was in hot pursuit behind her with his gun drawn. We all looked with disbelief at him. He looked at us, waved his gun at us and yelled, "Stay put or I'll blow your heads off." Then he quickly followed Jennifer. He disappeared behind the corner and then we heard the sounds of Jennifer resisting -- then pleading for her life -- "No! Oh no! Please don't!" Next we heard a loud gunshot blast -- and then another.

Several of us slowly approached the crime scene. We smelled the powder from the gun blasts -- and then we saw the two bodies -- and the blood. Jennifer was sitting on the floor, her head lodged in the corner of the wall with a bullet hole above her left ear. Her blue eyes were open -- seeing nothing. The blood flowed through her beautiful blond hair -- down over her ear and neck and onto her beige coat. Todd lay on the floor in his black coat surrounded by a pool of blood. His face was totally unrecognizable because he had apparently shot himself in his mouth. As one of the students went to call the police, blood continued to spread over the floor -- and later jelled. It was the most gruesome scene that I have ever witnessed.

In the next few days the murder/suicide became the big local story. According to what I heard on TV and read in the local newspapers, Jennifer was a graduate student in psychology. She was scheduled to receive her master's degree in June. I also learned that Todd was a detective with the Urbana Police Department. He had been on the police force for about twenty years.

Todd had met Jennifer when he was investigating a robbery that had occurred on campus. Despite the fact that Todd was a married man and a father of three young children, Jennifer had started seeing him. They apparently planned to marry after Todd had gotten a divorce. Over the Christmas break, Todd had traveled to Dayton, Ohio to meet Jennifer's parents. Then, everything changed. Jennifer decided to break off her engagement despite the fact that Todd had been granted a divorce. According to rumors on campus Jennifer's parents had urged her not to marry Todd because of the age difference and because they thought that he was going through a mid-life crisis. Apparently the break-up was too much for Todd to handle. He believed that he had given up everything for Jennifer. And, when he could not convince her to resume their affair, his love had turned into hate.

The local press seemed to side with Todd. They pictured Jennifer as a home wrecker and a person who played around with another person's feelings. The bad press even made me wonder about her -- especially how a psychology major could have allowed herself to get involved in such a relationship. I remember that one local newspaper story was particularly sentimental in its treatment of Todd. It went on about how he loved his family and how he enjoyed Christmas -- and how he had designed a mechanical tree stand that automatically turned the tree so that people could see all of the ornaments. It also included testimonials from Todd's fellow officers and Boy Scout masters about what a great guy he had been. It was a bit much. Nobody seemed to take Jennifer's side. Of course, I did not have access to what her home town newspaper was saying.

Looking back, it is obvious that a double standard was being applied -- and that the old stereotype of the wicked, scheming other woman was in play. When I talked with one student in the Psychology Department who had known Jennifer, he told me that she had been a very caring person who found herself in a bad situation. He said that she had tried to end the relationship with Todd in a mature manner but that he would have none of it. I guess today we would view him as having a fatal attraction. I found out that she even had gone to the Urbana Police Department to complain about his stalking her but got nowhere because of Todd's good relationship with the department.

The bloody murder scene left a lasting impression on all of us who witnessed it. The incident made us all aware of how fragile human relations are and how things can get out of control.

The 60th anniversary of that horrible event is coming up soon. One can only imagine all the wonderful things that Jennifer and Todd missed because of Todd's decision made in the heat of anger. What a waste! But, unfortunately, isn't that the story of the human condition? It is being repeated every day -- one murder after another. One wonders if it will ever end without some beneficent police state programming everyone in positive patterns of behavior through genetic engineering.

Compassion St.

Compassion

From an early age we are taught to show compassion for those having troubles and most of us do pretty well as long as it is the general body parts, but let it be the brain that is off and then it is much more common to show ridicule than compassion. This fact was piercingly brought to my attention last week when I went down to our afternoon tea.

Janet who is definitely showing dementia,
Came and started to sit near me until she spotted Lill
Who is also having problems: in sight, balance etc.
Janet started fussing about Lill and declared
"She shouldn't be out alone in the hall"
Finally after several false starts, Janet got up and left.
The rest of us seemed to silently heave a sigh of relief.
Not a one of us, including me, did anything to help her.
Then Lois came up in her electric scooter.
We all helped her maneuver into place.
Why did we not try to help Janet?
Is our fear of dementia partially because we know
We will be greeted with distain from others?

My Most Likable Boss

Like most of you I have had lots of jobs over the years -- and all sorts of bosses. The most likable boss that I ever had was a lady by the name of Mrs. Penn.

I became acquainted with her at the University of Illinois. I needed a job to help pay for my graduate work, and the U. of I. Student Employment Office sent me to Mrs. Penn to be interviewed for a position with The Human Relations Area File.

My interview lasted about one hour. At the end, Mrs. Penn told me that she wanted to hire me because I had extensive course work in the area of the humanities. Also, she was impressed by the fact that I had worked part time in the History and Political Science Library.

Mrs. Penn was a tiny, thin woman. She was in her mid-40s and had gray hair that was cut short with bangs. She used very little make-up and dressed in very plain blouses and dark-colored skirts. She needed glasses for reading. I remember that she had them attached to a metal chain so that she could hang them around her neck. She was constantly putting them on and off.

She had a smile like Mona Lisa's -- mysterious, sweet and earnest. If she laughed, which was often, she revealed teeth that had extensive dental work. Oh yes, another thing about her was that she was a chain smoker. She loved her Lucky Strikes which probably explained why her voice was low and gravelly.

She was very much a people person. She wanted us to know her as a individual -- not as a boss. She asked us to call her by her first name which was Rachel.

Every two hours we were given a fifteen minute break in addition to an hour off for lunch. The staff always took these breaks together. The library had its own cafeteria and lounge. We could take our lunch to the lounge if we wanted to or if the weather was nice go to a court yard that was near the cafeteria. It was during these breaks that Mrs. Penn consciously or unconsciously revealed a lot about herself, and we in turn shared a lot about ourselves with her.

I found out that Rachel's husband was a professor in the Sociology Department and had written several books. They had three children -- a son who was attending Harvard and two daughters who were enrolled at Urbana High School.

Mrs. Penn told us that she had been born into a Jewish family. Her people were Reformed Jews and as a child she had attended synagogue regularly. When she married, she converted to her husband's faith which was Quakerism. She admitted that she sometimes felt guilty about deserting Judaism. She related that recently she attended a synagogue with her mother and noticed how few people were there. She wondered why the attendance was so small. Then, it hit her. Many young Jewish people, like herself, had converted to other religions or had become agnostics or atheists.

Despite these occasional feelings of guilt, she assured us that she had found meaning in Quakerism. She said that her new faith had given her many good causes to fight for -- causes that promoted a more just and humane world.

She was the only boss I ever had who talked about the need for social action. She related that she and her husband had grown up during the 1930s and had been influenced by the liberalism of the New Deal. She told us about organizing groups to support unions, to defend the rights of minorities -- especially Blacks and Jews -- and to secure equal opportunity for women. She was especially proud of the fact that she had worked with Eleanor Roosevelt and other liberals on many causes.

Naturally, she told us about the social action groups within the university community and invited us to their meetings. I attended some. I guess the most unusual one involved going to a Friends meeting. I sat in silence with others until the spirit moved some to talk. Several talked about the need to help clothe, feed and care for the less fortunate.

I especially remember that Mrs Penn was very much against the use of violence to achieve ends -- even just ones. She believed, like Gandhi, that change could come about through economic, social and symbolic peaceful protest.

Another meeting that I attended involved a group that wanted Adlai Stevenson to run again for the presidency. Mrs. Penn had received a letter from Eleanor Roosevelt asking her to help organize a pro-Stevenson group on campus. I wasn't too enthusiastic about the whole thing since he had run two times before. Besides, there were new faces on the scene, such as Lyndon Johnson and John F. Kennedy, who wanted the nomination.

I remember that Mrs. Penn was upset by Kennedy gaining the nomination. She considered him a rich, spoiled young man who was where he was because of his father's money and influence.

Mrs. Penn was a very nurturing boss -- taking an interest in all our problems. She encouraged us to talk about everything from trying to prepare for tests to making ends meet financially to problems in our love lives. She welcomed every subject -- every difficulty. And, she offered good advice too.

She was very liberal for the times. For example, I remember an Egyptian student by the name of Mohammed Omar telling us about his problems dating American women. He told us all about his latest love and how she refused to have intercourse with him. He told us that in Egypt he was accustomed to having sex with a woman at least once a week at one of the many houses of prostitution in Alexandria.

His "regular party girl" had been a woman named Rosa. After enjoying a fine dinner and a stage show at the luxurious "house of pleasure," Rosa would guide him up to her bedroom to engage in an hour of love making. He paid $75.00 for each session. He said that he really missed the love making and that he couldn't understand why prostitution was not legal in the United States.

Well, after hearing all of this Mrs. Penn was so sympathetic -- expressing the hope that the American girl would eventually be willing to have sex with him. She said that she knew how important a physical union was to a relationship. Naturally, she did not defend the institution of prostitution. She tried to explain to Omar why the acceptance of such an institution exploited women and undermined their rights.

After I left the University of Illinois, I really didn't think much about Mrs. Penn until one day during the early '70s, I picked up a copy of **Life** magazine and started reading a piece written by a mother of a conscientious objector. She explained why her son refused to fight in Vietnam. I was surprised when I found out who had written the article. Yes, you guessed it -- it was Mrs. Penn. After finishing the article, I thought, "How like her."

All my other bosses pale in contrast to Mrs. Penn. Most of them were competent but went along with the "company image" of a boss. They seemed to fear revealing too much about themselves. Unlike Mrs. Penn they did not express their social and political opinions. Also, they refused to get too involved in our personal lives.

Mrs. Penn is probably gone by now. But, by remembering her in this piece, I'm helping to keep her memory alive -- and her example too. She was truly a likable boss --- and a remarkable human being. But, come to think about it, don't the two go together?

Teach St.

Brainwashing

Back in the 1950s and 1960s Americans were very concerned about brainwashing. We believed that the Chinese Reds had perfected the system of thought control and had used it on American soldiers captured in the Korean War. A popular film of the time was **The Manchurian Candidate** which featured brain control to the extreme. In the movie a captured American soldier is programmed to kill on command before his release.

In order to help students learn more about the dynamics of thought control, I used a Brainwashing Simulation. The game involved the need to recruit some "plants" to achieve the goals of the simulation.

I and other members of the Humanities Teaching Team played the simulation in connection with our unit on Red China. Mao's little red book entitled, **Quotations From Chairman Mao Tse-tung** was read by students to understand Mao's belief that everyone should think alike. Also, students read some articles about the actual process of thought control used by the Chinese. We discussed the need for the leaders of thought control to have "plants" to help them expose those who were guilty of non-communistic thinking. The "plants" would denounce the capitalistic thinking individuals and help them see the error of their ways. In doing this, the "plants" helped bring about "thought reform."

The simulation was played without telling the students that it was going to be played. Before the game we recruited at least eight students to be "plants."

The simulation started by the teaching team claiming that the administration did not like the way the class was being conducted and had insisted on the following new rules being followed:

1. Students are forbidden to go off campus to eat lunch.

2. Students will no longer be able to go on field trips.
3. Students must not do crafts during class time.
4. Students must not stand by the door before the bell rings.
5. Students must not bring snacks with them to class.

We asked the students to express their views about the new rules. We told them that we would like to tell the administration that they would abide by the new rules.

Well, a lot of students voiced strong objections to the new rules. Others remained silent. Some demanded to confront the administrators who had proposed the new rules. I remember one saying, "They are trying to take all the freedom and fun out of this class. I don't want to be part of it if it is going to like all the other boring classes in this building. Tell Mr. Knight (our principal) that we would like to talk to him about these new rules."

Then, the "plants" started putting pressure on everyone to accept the rules. They said things like the following:

"Let's admit it, we have been doing a lot of silly things in this class. We have been wasting a lot of time and fooling around too much. I myself have been guilty of a lot of silliness. I have taken advantage of the freedom that I have been given in this class."

"I have been knitting too much in class. I know that this distracts our attention from the lesson."

"I have often been late getting back to class after going off campus for lunch. I admit that I lack a lot of self-discipline."

"I admit that I bring candy to class and like to share it with my friends. I know that this interfers with the lesson."

Well, the other students couldn't believe what they were hearing. They could not believe that some of the "plants" would admit to any wrong doing. The "plants" stuck to their guns and told everyone that they had seen "the error of their ways and hoped that everyone else would too." In one class a "plant" declared, "I think that these new rules are great. They will give us the discipline and structure that we need. We all have to admit that we haven't been able to handle in a positive way the freedoms that we have been given in this class. I can see why the administration is upset."

When any of the students in the class declared that they did not want the class changed, they were quickly denounced. The "plants" said things like the following:

"Now, Ben, you know that you have not taken this class seriously. When was the last time you got back to class on time after lunch?"

"Bill, the only things that you do on field trips is to talk too much and cause trouble for the docents."

"Come on Judy, admit it, you never take a note in this class. All you do is talk, eat and work on that latch-hook project of yours. Admit it, you can't handle the freedom."

After the heated and freewheeling discussion we asked the class to vote on the new rules. And, believe it or not, every time we played the game the new rules were adopted.

After the vote, I or one of the other teachers would suddenly stand up and yell: "Thanks comrades! All Power to the Chinese People!"

Then the "plants" on cue would stand up and yell, "All Power to The People's Republic of China! Hail, Comrade Mao Tse-tung!"

A lengthy discussion followed the simulation. As you can imagine, those not in on it -- those who were fooled -- were at first very angry. Then, as we explained why we had done it, they calmed down. We asked them to express the feelings that they had experienced at certain points in the simulation. They testified to the power of the group in the brainwashing process. They said that the "confessions" made by the "plants" were especially effective in changing their minds.

This exercise in brainwashing and thought control was very effective. It was something that students remembered for a long time. In the mid-90s I recall meeting one of my former students and talking about Humanities. One of the things that she remembered was playing the thought control simulation.

Generally, I found the simulation to be a very effective teaching tool. I played another one on revolution and class conflict that was also very effective. I plan to write about it in a future piece.

Flash Mobs

The other day as I watched The Early Morning Show a feature appeared about a supposedly unusual phenomenon called "flash mobs." I use the word "supposedly" because to me it is simply a part of or a variation of "street theatre" that has been around for a long time.

In the case of "flash mobs," a group of people (about 20 to 35) suddenly and unexpectedly appear in a public place and engage in some type of activity. In some cases words or slogans will be spoken as the people engage in their physical exercises. Usually the so-called "mob" is trying to make a point about some social issue or aspect of daily life.

When I was team teaching in a course called Humanities at Webster Groves High School back in the '70s, the drama teacher, Mrs. Ernestine Smizer, taught us all (both teachers and students) about street theatre and then supervised actual "street happenings." This came only after giving us the fundamentals of drama and doing improvisations.

One of the aspects of street theatre is that nobody should know about what is going to happen until the event. According to Ernestine that was the only way it would be effective and truely a pure form of the concept of street theatre. This, of course, eventually got her into trouble with the our principal, Mr. Jerry Knight ("Mr. Cool") who met every challenge with extraordinary wisdom.

The first spontaneous happening occurred in the two rest rooms on the first floor which were located near the front entrance. During the break between classes, students found that the signs on the doors of the restrooms had been changed. Both were marked with signs saying "Co-Ed Restroom." They also saw numerous boys and girls (students or "actors" from our Humanities class) going into and out of the restrooms. Well, you can imagine the reaction. It put people in a state of shock. While some simply stood with their mouths open, others were pointing and yelling, "Look what they are doing!" By the way Ernestine thought that event was one of the most successful dramatic happenings that she had ever directed. Indeed, she gave all the students who participated in the happening "As"

While Ernestine was delighted with what had happened, Jerry wasn't. He immediately called the Humanities team to the office and demanded to know what we were up to. Ernestine wasn't a bit intimidated by Jerry's request. In fact, I remember Ernestine telling the rest of us before the meeting, "Now don't worry. The man just needs to be educated about street theatre. Once he understands, he will go along with it." Well, it didn't entirely work out that way.

During the meeting Ernestine explained to Jerry that she was only using street theatre as a teaching method to help students become more confident about using various techniques of drama. She also explained to him that street theatre was often used to bring attention to public issues. In fact, she said the students in he recent dramatic happening were only highlighting how ridiculous it is to have so much separation of the sexes in daily activities.

I have to give Jerry credit for at least hearing out Ernestine's explanation. However, after she finished, he remained largely unconvinced. While he allowed us continue to use street theatre as a teaching method, he insisted that we keep him informed about when and where we intended to supervise the next dramatic happening. Of course, we had no choice but to accept his demands.

Of course, Ernestine wasn't too happy about Jerry's restrictions. I can still hear her declare, "Well, what can one expect from a former math teacher."

The next event took place in the cafeteria during the lunch hour. It was centered on what had happened in one of the restrooms on the second floor. A restroom had recently been painted by a group of students who were interested in improving the school. They had decided that it would be nice besides repainting the walls to paint a mural on one of them. They settled on a lovely pastoral scene.

Unfortunately, shortly after the job had been completed, several students vandalized the painting. As a result, the administration ordered the janitors to paint over the entire mural. Naturally, the students who had painted it were very upset because they were willing to paint another.

The dramatic event, which of course this time Jerry knew about, involved a funeral service for the wall with the mural. It took place in the cafeteria and then the court yard.

While students and teachers were in the mist of eating lunch, a long line of Humanities students appeared bearing a black casket. They paraded the casket through out the cafeteria and then went to the court yard for the burial.

A student by the name of Mike Wallace had written a eulogy for the event. It was so unusual and well done that I kept it among my teaching souvenirs. I should mention that Mike was dressed like a priest as he read it. Here it is:

"Dearly beloved we are gathered together in this lovely setting in the presence of God and these witnesses to pay a last tribute to the late and beloved Mr. John Wall of restroom 201.

"Those of you who knew him, know that he was a strong and beautiful wall. He was created by the loving and artistic hands of Webster Groves students. The artistic designs which filled him, won him many friends and much admiration. He will be greatly missed.

"In the prime of his life he was cut down by evil hands. John did nothing to warrant such brutal treatment. He was here only to give joy and pleasure. Instead, he was cut down in the bloom of his youth by insensitive neurotics. While we feel sorry for the persons who committed this senseless act, we can't forgive their motives.

"Our hearts go out to John's widow -- the East Wall-- and his lovely children -- the North and South Walls of restroom 201.

"It is our sincere hope that John has not died in vain. Let his death symbolize the need for mankind to care for beautiful things and to respect the rights of others to enjoy beauty.

"We commit his spirit to the Great Wall in the Sky. May John find peace and everlasting life in the spirit of the Great Wall.

"We now commit his remains to the Earth, from which he came. Ashes to ashes, dust to dust, and wall to wall. Amen!" Then other members of the funeral party sharted shouting, "Amen! Amen! Amen!"

The reaction to the funeral was one of surprise and awe. I can still remember seeing expressions of disapproval on the faces of many staff members who were trying to eat lunch. I'm sure some were thinking, "What is that crazy Ernestine up to now?" However, the students generally seemed fascinated with the event. Many accompanied the funeral party outside to the court yard and joined in with the "Amens."

Other dramatic happenings occurred throughout the year. The students certainly gained confidence in expressing themselves through drama. They also learned that street theatre can be a powerful tool to educated the public about social issues.

Needless to say, I'm all for "flash mobs" and look forward to more accounts of their occurrences. I only wish that the media people would educate themselves about street theatre and its long history in making a positive contribution to human society.

The Gift Of The Buddha

The other day as I packed nicknacks in preparation to move to another apartment, I came across a ten-inch tall statue of Buddha and my mind was immediately flooded with memories of some remarkable students.

The statue is very heavy because it is chiseled out of red granite. I sometimes use it as a paperweight. After I picked it up, I found myself looking at it closely. I noticed the blissful expression on the Buddha's face which verified that he had truly reached Enlightenment. Then, I turned the Buddha upside down and found the following names printed on a small piece of paper: Alicia LaChance, Brehnan Collins, Ross Nowel, Craig Shohl and Kathy Nameth. They were the students who had given me the statue back in 1989 shortly before they graduated from Webster Groves High School. I remembered that after they gave me the statue that I always referred to them as the "devotees of the Buddha."

They were all enrolled in 20th Century International Literature and Affairs which I team taught with an English teacher by the name of Pat Whitington. As I read each name, the image of each came into my mind. While they all were different in terms of physical appearance and ability, they were all interested in learning and very much aware of social and political issues.

They all knew that I was into the study of Eastern religions -- especially Hinduism and Buddhism. Some of them had taken my section of World History as 10th graders where I really enjoyed introducing students -- in most cases for the first time -- to contrasting philosophies and religions. They also knew that I collected Buddhas because I displayed my collection in my classroom. I must have had at least ten Buddhas in various sizes and poses scattered throughout my room. They were either on my desk or my file cabinets or book cases.

My appreciation for the Buddha was widely known throughout the school too. That fact was brought home to me one day as I walked down the hall. I overheard one student whispering to another, "There goes the Buddha man." That might also explain the practice of many students, who in some cases I never knew, coming into my classroom to rub Buddha's tummy for good luck. This especially happened during finals.

Shortly after giving me the statue, the "devotees of the Buddha" did another remarkable thing. They decided to protest what was happening to the Chinese students and workers in Tiananmen Square. You will recall that in April of 1989, Chinese students had demanded political reforms. Student demonstrators camped out in Tiananmen Square, Beijing in a major peaceful protest. Some 100,000 students and workers marched and at least twenty other cities saw protests. In response, martial law was imposed and the army troops crushed the demonstrations in and around Tiananmen Square on June 3-4. The estimate of the death toll was between 500 to 7,000. At least 10,000 dissidents were arrested and 31 people were tried and executed.

The "devotees of the Buddha" decided to show their contempt for the Chinese government by wearing black arm bands and circulating a petition asking President George H. Bush to take action to safeguard the rights of the students.

As head of the social studies department, I was required to wear a robe and sit with the administrators during graduation ceremonies. So, on the night of June 7, I was there when "the devotees of the Buddha" received their diplomas. As each of them came to the stage, I could see that they still were wearing their black arm bands. I remember being filled with admiration for their action and thinking that they were putting into use -- both in terms of thought and action -- their education.

Today as I look at the Buddha, I realize that I not only received a gift of a statue but memories of some unforgettable students and their decision to protest an act of political and social injustice.

I have often wondered what happened to "the devotees of the Buddha." Hopefully, they are still enjoying learning, still taking a stand and still trying to make a better world. In my heart of hearts, I know that they are doing all three.

Buddha has reached enlightenment

Coping St.

Coping With The Flower Children Generation

Pat's account of coping with her teenage children in the 60's and 70's caused me to remember my teaching experiences with that unique group of individuals -- the so-called "flower children." It was very difficult meeting their "needs" -- or should I say their "demands." At Webster Groves High students often backed up their "requests" with demonstrations -- picketing in front of the building, student walkouts, and marches to the principal's office where they would chant, "We will overcome" or "Change it! Change it!" Naturally, they usually had called one or all of the local TV stations before the demonstration. Mr. Jerry Knight ("Mr. Cool") was our principal at the time and he me the challenges with extraordinary wisdom.

They certainly shook us up and forced a lot of changes in the educational system. I remember very vividly the principal getting on the intercom and exclaiming, "Everything is under control. I'm handling the situation. Teachers, continue the lessons that you have planned for the period. Students, continue to remain in class and follow the instructions of your teachers." Meantime you could hear the shouting and chanting echoing up the stairwells and throughout the building. The whole experience was too much for many older administrators and teachers; they could not adjust to the demand for changes and decided to retired early.

Generally, I feel that many of the changes that the "flower children" wanted were long overdue and were positive. The following is a list of complaints from the so-called "flower children" and how we tried at Webster Groves High School to meet them.

"This stuff isn't relevant today." They were talking about a lot of the general survey courses -- from U.S. History to American Literature to World History. They were concerned with Vietnam, with poverty in America, with racism, with civil liberties, and with the environment. Gradually, we increased the number of courses that dealt with contemporary issues. In history courses the teachers connected up the past with contemporary concerns. In the case of the English Department more contemporary literature was included in survey courses. In the science area there was an attempt to include issues concerning the environment and medical ethics into general science courses. Also, many teachers encouraged students to become involved in community types of projects.

"Boring -- everything is so boring in class." This was a common complaint. In desperation most of us tried to find and try out new methods. So you had the inquiry approach, the use of more visuals, cooperative learning techniques, community involvement, interdisciplinary courses like American Studies and Humanities and lots of field trips, role-playing exercises, simulations, moral dilemma exercises, a wide choice of projects and outside speakers.

Also, there for awhile we tried all kinds of 9-week courses as alternatives to survey courses. In social studies we offered courses like You And The Law, U.S. Medical Care, and The American Indian. The English Department went the same direction. Hence you found such courses as The American Film, Non-Violent Literature, War and Peace, Peaches and Cream and Mysteries and Detective Stories. Also, the administration changed the graduation requirements -- allowing students more choice in what they took. There were some negatives to these "reforms." General knowledge wasn't always repeated enough. The 3 R's were neglected. Visuals were stressed over writing and discussion. Some basic courses such as World History were dropped as requirements. Hence, even today members of the "flower children" generation -- and as far as that goes those that followed -- often have gaps in their knowledge. They haven't heard about some basic information that we the members of the older generation consider essential.

"I feel excluded." This especially came from the African-American students. But it later came to include women, gays and students who came from multi-cultural backgrounds. Special so-called Black History courses were offered. Later, special courses about women were created. We also made sure that we planned events for Black History Month and National Women's History Month. A greater effort was made to include the contributions of Blacks and women into general survey courses. When it came to student groups, there for awhile quotas were worked out so that enough Black students would be cheerleaders, on the student council, and in the choir.

"Students have rights too and especially the right to protest." This lead to the administration working out complex procedures to deal with discipline and bringing grievances to the attention of the administration. Also, information about students had to be more carefully monitored. Many times counselors would not share things about a student with teachers for fear of violating his/her right to privacy.

"Don't you trust us?" This lead to all kinds of so-called "reforms." Students were given more free time to interrelate -- to find themselves -- to show that they could develop self-discipline. It led to peer counseling, the principal forming a panel of students to advise him, students monitoring designated "smoking areas" and some teachers allowing students to elect members of the class to work with them in creating units. While some of these reforms worked well, others did not. Many students never could handle unstructured time very well.

"Can we also fully participate in all sports?" Of course, this involved female students who felt that they should also be treated equally when it came to sports. At Webster Groves this became quite an issue -- especially with regard to the money that was being spent on boys versus girls P.E. Over the years every effort was made to provide equality of opportunity.

"The dress code is too strict and outdated." This led to dropping most dress guidelines except that a person had to wear shoes for health and safety. When some students decided to wear Halloween costumes, there was quite a "crisis" about it on the part of the faculty. Finally, the costumes were prohibited as a distraction. What was allowed was certain types of dress days (Western, the 50's, casual) in which both students and teachers were encouraged to participate. Every once in a while there would be a concern about attire. There for awhile some students were wearing jeans with holes in them -- in some cases in the butt and genital areas. This led to a crack down on such attire.

"The grading system is elitist and racist." This led to several revisions in the grading system. Teachers were encouraged -- indeed required to include more factors in the grading process. The number of African-Americans receiving low grades was carefully monitored. The concept of requiring teachers to exhibit a bell shaped grading curve was ignored.

While some of these reforms were necessary, I feel that the standards were lowered too much. Grade inflation was the result. Often students would go off to college with high grade averages and find themselves being placed in remedial English and failing the first year. They were not being properly prepared.

"We feel that the fine arts have been neglected." This complaint lead to an increase in art, drama and music courses. It also lead to having a Fine Arts Festival for one week out of the year. All kinds of things were planned -- action painting events, foreign films, display of student art, presentation by musical groups, and "drama happenings" or "street theatre." The latter caused a lot of anxiety for the administration and consternation on the part of the more conservative faculty members. Once Mrs. Smizer the drama teacher directed students in a happening that involved turning several bathrooms into ones for both sexes. Another involved a mock funeral with coffin, a procession of mourners, and a tongue-in-cheek eulogy for Mr Fuddy-duddy -- meaning tradition and old, outdated ideas. As I recall the "burial" took place in the courtyard. It was done without any announcement (According to Mrs. Smizer, "It would have spoiled the surprise and gone against the very concept of a "drama happening.") in the cafeteria during the busy second lunch period. Well, as you can imagine, the principal was not amused. But the times were such that Mrs. Smizer got her way and the principal actually backed down. She did agree to tip him off about future happenings. But, that was it. No other restriction was imposed. The biggest negative about the week was that nothing else got done. After ten years, the festival was dropped. Students were leaving the building in large numbers and not attending the many events.

"You teachers do not understand us." This lead to all kinds of awareness workshops. Here are a few: feminism, the Black student, drugs and alcoholism, student rights and sex education. These plus the ones on new educational methods kept us all very busy during the summers. We, of course, were encouraged to enroll in courses that would also help us understand this challenging generation.

After writing this paper, I realize why I was so burned out after teaching at Webster Groves High School for twenty-six years. I feel exhausted just writing about it. I think I'll take a nap.

Ten Memorable Students

One of the things that I have missed in teaching is the opportunity to encounter students who possess unique characteristics or views that provide variety, challenge and excitement in my own life. Here are some distinctive individuals that came into my mind as I closed my eyes and thought about memorable students that I have met.

Dolly - The Silent Protester

She protested the war in Vietnam in quiet ways in keeping with her shy, introspective nature. She always wore a black arm band and dressed in long flowing flowered dresses on her petite figure. She always managed secretively to leave the peace sign somewhere close to where she had been sitting. She would print it on the blackboard with chalk, or tape it to the wall or form it out of gum and then stick it on the side of a table or file cabinet. Inbetween classes one would see her scurrying down the long hallways, giving the peace sign to anti-war buddies and handing out flyers about some anti-war rally.

Margie -- The Genetics Expert

She was striking with her blond hair, blue eyes and outgoing friendly manner. She was a very intelligent student -- especially in science. She was very concerned with the danger of passing on bad genes. She herself was a carrier of a bad gene that might result in a serious eye disorder for any children born to her. She wondered aloud if she should have children. The matter weighed heavily upon her. She often argued with other students about the need for the government to regulate who should be allowed to have children. She felt that every effort should be made to stop perpetuating negative genes.

Larry - The Frederick Douglass of Webster Groves High School

While Larry was average in height, his muscular body and classic African face allowed him to dominate any group. He organized the Students for Black Awareness and Action and attracted quite a large following. He denounced the way in which Blacks had been treated in Webster Groves and called for reforms. He published an underground newspaper called **The Dark Side** which became more popular than the regular high school paper. It even had book and movie reviews in it plus some cartoons. The administration had a terrible time trying to stop it from being distributed in the school.

Susan -- Miss Hickey

She was a very tall (6'2") red head with freckles who was in one of my senior U.S. Government classes. She was in love with being in love. She was always wanting to talk to me about her latest date which I found rather unusual. Most teenagers keep such things to themselves or share the details with other teenagers. Anyway, she always liked to prove to me that she was one of the "movers" on campus by showing me her latest hickey. It was usually on her neck -- on the right side. One time, much to my amazement she raised her skirt and showed me one that was located on her upper thigh. I often wondered if she had pinched herself in such a way as to leave a mark that resembled a hickey. I'll never know. I only know that "the hickey evidence" left a lasting impression on me.

Beth - Miss Anti-Social

She was one of the most disturbed students that I have ever met and one of the most frustrating to deal with. Outwardly she looked cute with her slim figure, page-boy haircut and baby face. Inwardly, there hid a demon. She totally distrusted people and needed to strike out at them. I never saw her speak to anyone in a friendly way. If you would address her, she often would not answer. She used silence as a way to strike out. She had truly mastered the art of passive aggression. She especially enjoyed putting people down -- especially adults who tried to reach out to her. I have often wondered what ever became of her. Once I met a professor from Webster University who told me about one of his most difficult students. Guess who it was. Yes, you guessed it. It was Beth. She had struck again.

Latasha -Miss Africa

She came from the inner city and was a very tall girl -- about 6' -- with the classic features of someone from central Africa -- now highlighted by her Afro. She was very intelligent, outspoken and proud of her African heritage. She was instrumental in bringing out into the open many issues that troubled Blacks within their own community. She was very outspoken about being discriminated against by other Blacks because she was so black -- so African.

In our many heated discussions in a class entitled "American Problems" Latasha threw out the opening gauntlet. She could be very confrontational. I vividly remember her proclaiming, "In American society the lighter you are the more preference you are shown. No wonder so many of my Black brothers and sisters want to be white. Many Blacks here at Webster dislike me because I am so representative of mother Africa. They will not allow me to join their groups. They do not even want to be seen speaking to me for fear that it will turn off their white friends."

She was also very critical about Black men wanting to date white women. One day she said angrily, "You Black men have been brainwashed by the white dominated society to believe that African women are not beautiful. You want white women -- especially those that have Nordic characteristics -- I'm talking about the blonde, blue-eyed creatures that dominate the world of advertising. Well, I'm here to tell you that I'm an African woman and I'm Black and beautiful." I vividly remember that she did not stop there but continued by naming specific Black men in the class who were or had been dating white women. They were really put on the grill as they found themselves being denounced not only by Latasha but by all the Black girls in class.

Latasha also spoke out about the treatment of inner city Black students by Blacks living in Webster Groves. She declared, "You think that we are trash from the slums don't you? You think that you're better than us because you live in Webster Groves and have been accepted by the whites. Well, I'm here to tell you that your fooling yourselves. North Webster is still the slave quarters for the hired help of Webster Groves."

Latasha could certainly spark lively discussions about racial issues. Her outspoken remarks caused heated discussions and were without a doubt some of the most explosive and yet necessary discussions that I can remember having with students. I remember really having to work to keep the lid on the emotions and to remind students to let each person speak and to listen to each other. In the give and take exchange I know that I learned a lot and the students did too -- not only about race issues but how to discuss hot topics in a meaningful and constructive way We were all challenged to think differently by an outspoken girl from the inner city.

Cathy - Miss "You Have To Like Me"

She was a very intelligent student and a very attractive one with her slim figure, auburn hair and blue eyes. However, she felt that nobody would like her unless she did something for them -- like writing a term paper for them or doing their home work. If you put her in a group, she would usually do the work for each member of the group. I found that I really had to watch her. She even had worked out a system of signals to give students answers to questions during tests. I finally had to complain to the principal and the sponsor of the local chapter of the National Honor Society (Cathy was a member) about the fact that she was helping others cheat. She was one of the most pathetic students that I can recall. So smart and yet so insecure.

Anne - The Tragic Cheerleader

While Anne was very petite, she made up for it by her school spirit. She could lead cheers with more enthusiasm than anybody else that I can remember. She often appeared representing the Webster Statesmen by wearing a tux and a top hat and carrying a cane. She seemed to have so much energy and pep. But, I noticed in class that she also had terrible mood swings. The middle of the road was never where Anne was. If she was happy she wasn't just happy, she was ecstatic. And, when she was sad, she was sadder than anybody in the whole wide world. After she graduated she committed suicide for a love affair that had ended. She shot herself in the head. So tragic. I was told that she had tried to seek help for her drug and alcohol addiction but something must have gone terribly wrong. Why anyone trusted her with a gun for self-defense I'll never know. I have visited her vault several times at Resurrection Cemetery and always wondered if someone could have prevented what happened. She has missed so much by dying so young.

Elana - Miss Focused

Elana was born in Germany and then had come to the United States with her parents. She was quite intelligent in all academic areas. She spoke several languages and knew exactly what she wanted. She wanted to major in international studies and someday return to Germany. She took every college bound course and did very well in each of them. I had her in Honors American Studies. By the way she was also very attractive and well adjusted. She had a very outgoing, warm personality. One day she came to me and told me that she was going to enter a contest in order to get a full scholarship to any college of her choice in Germany. She had to write an essay about Germany and the prospects for its future. This was before Germany was reunited. She wrote the essay and then had me read it to make suggestions. I did and then she submitted the revised version of her essay. Well, she won. So, at the age of 18 she was off to attend a university in Germany and major in international studies. Quite an extraordinary girl -- so focused, so determined, so attractive, so intelligent and so well-adjusted.

Emily -- The Girl With A Heavy Christian Conscience

She was a student in Humanities -- a team taught course in which I was involved. As part of a unit on India we included the study of Hinduism and Buddhism. The teachers thought that a role-playing exercise would be a way to help students to learn the material. The exercise involved a confrontation between a group of Buddhist monks and Christian missionaries. The exercise was designed to explore all the differences and similarities between the two religions. Students where asked to wear costumes. Emily was assigned to play a Buddhist monk. She along with others appeared wearing saffron robes and holding beggar's bowls. The exercise seemed to go well -- at least the teachers thought so. Well, the next day in comes Emily quite upset. She was very concerned about the fact that she had played the role of a Buddhist monk. She felt that as a sincere Christian she should not have done so. She wondered if she had under minded the faith that other students had in Christ. Well, everything was tabled so that we could talk about it. We had a so-called fish-bowl discussion where students would sit in a circle and if they wanted to contribute to the discussion they would pull their chairs into the center of the circle. Anyway, after a two hour exchange, we were able to help Emily feel better about the experience and to reassure her that her role-playing had not under minded any student's conviction to be a follower of Jesus.

I'm going to stop now. I'm sure that other memorable students will come to mind. But, the ones I have mentioned certainly reflect the variety of students that I taught and the unexpected daily life of a teacher.

Love St.

Nothing Like Being In Love With Love

I love being in love with love.
    Why? Because:
        the heart beats faster,
        the mind become dizzy,
        one becomes ticklish,
        and you find that you giggle a lot
    and you do the most zany things.
It comes in stages.
        First, one becomes attracted to another's lips, hair, ass, eyes, manner,
        personality.
        Then, comes the first touch.
        It's like being hit by lightning.
        That leads to the first kiss -- then touching nipples, face, penis,
        vulva — licking and sucking G-spots . Often the lovers are joined
        by others for rimming and performing cunnilingus.
        Then comes the interlocking of the naked bodies-- followed by the
        rush of ecstasy as all the lovers reach climax.

Where does it take place?
        On a dance floor
            or in a shower
        or under soft blankets,
        or in the backseat of a car
        or anywhere -- anytime.

What emotions result in this passion of ecstasy?
        Here is a list:

feelings of oneness,
complete physical pleasure,
light headedness,
promising anything,
spiritual bonding and
BEING IN HEAVEN.

Oh, there is nothing like finding another or others who is/are willing to love, love, love --YOU AND ONLY YOU.

And it can happen between a man and a woman, a man and a man, a woman and a woman, and yes in threesomes and groupies of same or mixed sexes.

Oh, there is nothing like falling in love with LOVE.

Love - To Cherish Most Dear

Was Mom Bisexual?

After hearing my title, you're probably thinking, "Come on Bud. Now really! Isn't anything sacred? Are you trying to shock us again?"

In response to those thoughts, I want to declare here and now that I am serious. I really would like an answer to the question. And since you are all sophisticated women of the world, you might be able to give me the answer to it after hearing the evidence.

The question came to my mind as a result of reading about so many famous women writers who were either lesbians or bisexuals. The latest biography that I read was about Edna St. Vincent Millay who carried on with both men and women. By the way, her husband understood -- indeed embraced the idea of complete sexual freedom for his beloved.

Now let's get to my mother. I'm beginning to think that she had a long standing affair with a woman by the name of Dorothy or "Dotti" Garst.

As proof I want to tell you about my memories of the two of them together. As a child I was often in the car when the two "flappers" took off for a lark to shop, visit friends, have lunch and see a movie. As I recall, they both loved to see films featuring Joan Crawford and Carol Lombard. During these outings, I listened as they chatted about their concerns and shared tears, hugs and kisses.

I remember my mother being fascinated with Dorothy and wanting to imitate her. In fact, Mom even changed her first name from Irene to Dorothy shortly after meeting Dotti.

As I look at old pictures of them during the late 1920s and early 1930s, I can't say that Dotti was especially pretty. Attractive yes, but not beautiful. She was considered tall at 5'9" for that time period. I remember that not everyone liked her personality. She was friendly enough but seemed to be holding back -- probably due to her innate shyness. While her voice had a pleasant sound to it, she seemed to speak slowly -- carefully -- as if trying to avoid offending anyone. She was a good listener. If you were speaking to her, her blue eyes would look attentively at you. You felt that you had her full attention. Besides loving to go to movies, she read fashion magazines with a passion.

One photo that goes back to 1928 shows Dotti with brunette hair that had been bobbed and wearing glasses. She is smiling at the person taking the photograph. It is a smile that reveals teeth that are really too prominent.

The one thing that I learned early about her was that she was ambitious. She was determined to make something of her life. She wanted more -- more money, more travel, more status, more excitement.

Dotti had been raised on a truck farm outside the little farming town of Milan, Illinois. I remember Mom and Dotti going out to the farm several times to visit Dotti's parents. Mom would often buy produce from them for canning. I remember meeting Dotti's parents -- hardy rustic, hard-working people. Looking back, I can understand why Dotti wanted something better than the strenuous life of a farmer.

Dotti had married young after she graduated from high school -- to get away from farm life -- and to find happiness. Well, she didn't get very far. Her husband Jack worked at one of the John Deere plants on the assembly line. While he was an attractive guy, he wasn't great in bed. "Wham, bang, thank you ma'am" describes his ability as a lover. I remember that Mom told Dotti that my dad often came too fast too and then then fell asleep. Both women wanted romance along with the sex. I gathered that they would have preferred their husbands to be more like Ronald Coleman or Gary Grant.

While my mother thought she had to continue with her marriage because of her children, Dotti didn't. She did not have any little ones to worry about -- and didn't want any. It was obvious that Dotti did not think that happiness for a woman meant a husband and children.

Dotti decided to attend one of the local beauty schools and become a hair stylist. She turned out to be an outstanding student and after graduation was hired at the Purple Lily Beauty Parlor.

It was during this time that Dotti used her knowledge of make-up, hair, clothes and body language to transform herself into a more attractive woman. She also gained a lot of confidence as she did her work. She often told Mom how to dress, how to style her hair, what color to tint it and how to walk and sit gracefully. Mom took her advice seriously and soon she was looking like Dotti. Perhaps unconsciously, both had transformed themselves into their ideal of what a Hollywood star should be like.

In a photo taken during this time Mom is pictured next to Dotti. They are standing very close and are smiling -- not at the camera but at each other.

As the years went by the two women became as close as sisters. On many of their trips when I would go with them during the summer before school started, the two of them would talk about their problems with their husbands, birth control, their hopes for the future, and yes their affection for each other. There would be tears, comforting hugs and on many occasions in the privacy of the car kisses.

Dotti eventually divorced Jack and set out on her own. She decided to move to Tampa, Florida where she quickly got a job at one of the leading beauty parlors. Mom and Dotti exchanged letters all the time. Mom seemed to be fascinated with Dotti's courage to make her own living and to go to new places. I think that Mom secretly wished she could have a different life too.

Dotti's letters were filled with happenings in and around Tampa. She related how she had taken up golf in order to meet rich and successful people -- especially men -- at the local country clubs. While she dated many men, she never married. Besides signing her letters with "love and hugs," Dotti would also leave the impressions of her lips too. Mom signed her letters to Dotti the same way.

Dotti eventually opened up her own beauty salon with the backing of some of her new friends. It was called The Tropical Palms. She was very successful. Evenutally, she hired and supervised ten employees in her shop.

Once in a while she would return to visit friends in Moline. She seemed like a VIP to me because Mom insisted on treating her as such. The whole family would meet Dotti at the train station. She usually stayed at our house in one of the guest bedrooms. During her stay we had lots of steaks because Dotti liked them so much. As Dad worked during the day, the two women used his car to make visits to old friends, to shop, to lunch out and to exchange confidences.

In my Mom's mind Dotti became the ultimate liberated woman -- one who had created a life on her terms. Over the years, Mom would receive photos of Dotti with one of her new rich boyfriends or a new formal, or with a new hair style. Eventually she even sent a photo of herself after getting a face lift. Meanwhile in response, Mom would send Dotti pictures of her grown children, her grandchildren and even her great-grandchildren.

Over time Mom seemed to settle for the life that fate had given her. Indeed, she was happy and proud of her achievements as a wife, mother and grandmother. At the same time she respected Dotti for the life she had chosen. She recognized that Dotti had gotten all the things that she had wanted --- plenty of money, status, clothes and men. By the way many of her lovers stayed with her -- caring for her -- for many years. The relationships remind one of Jackie Kennedy's relationships with several older men toward the end of her life.

When my mother died in 1993, among the condolences was a beautiful sympathy card from Dotti in which she declared how much she had loved my mother. And get this. She had signed it and kissed it -- leaving the imprint of her lips.

A Menage A Trois

I went to
        a massage parlor
and fell in love
        with the two owners
        who came from
            Sweden

When I went in
        for the treatment,
I had no idea that
        I would become
deeply involved with
        what they call
A MENAGE A TROIS.
        But I did and
it was wonderful.

The parlor was
        operated by
Brunhilda and Kunther
        Swanson.

At first I thought
        they were a married
couple and then
        found out they were

brother and sister.

Both were trim and
        muscular, blonde --with
blue eyes and bright
        welcoming smiles.

I had some difficulty
        understanding their
accent but soon adjusted and
        found their English
cute and charming.

When I started going
        I had Kunther for my
treatments.

I would strip
        and lay on a table
that had a soft blue pad
        on it.

Kunther would start
        the treatments with
hot towels to relax the
        muscles and open up
the pores of my skin.

After that he would
        gently remove the
towels and use his hands
        to massage:
        neck
        shoulders
        chest
        waist
        buttocks

        thighs
        legs
        feet.
He must have had a foot fetish
        because when he got
to my feet, he would gently
        suck and kiss
each toe.

        After he finished the
        back side,
he would gently turn
        me on my back and
work on the front side
        of my body.

During the treatment
        he would ask again and again,
"Does that feel good?"
        I always said, "Ah, yes!"

When he got to your cock
        and balls, he would
use a small hot towel to
        twirl them around
a bit.

Then, he would ask, "Does that
        relax your manhood?"
I always replied, "Ah yes, it
        feels wonderful."

He was very happy to hear that
        and said that I had
experienced his own maneuver
        which he invented.

He called it the Kunther Twril."

During each treatment,
        he enjoyed chatting with me.
He asked about my occupation, interests,
        and marriage status.

At the end of the session,
        he always brought in the
hot bamboo sticks for
        gently beating the back and
        the buttocks.

Then, one day I found that
        his sister Brunhilda
was going to do the treatment.
        She went through the
same step by step therapy
        with gentle skill.

I have to admit that when she
        did the "Kunther Twril"
I got a heart on my cock. But
        she just smiled and
commented, "Oh what a compliment!"

I finally asked her out for a
        date and we would up at
her place in her bedroom making
        passionate love.

Wow, making love to her was
        fantastic. She had a
vagina, with muscles that
        could tighten or
expand to give your cock

a glorious feel.

This went on for months. Then,
        once Kunther appeared.
Yes, he opened the bedroom door
        and smiled as he saw me
humping his sister.

He said softly, "May I join in
        with the fun?"
Without hesitation, we both
        said, "Sure, welcome aboard."
I guess that we were in such a
        state of bliss that we wanted
to share the experience.
        Besides, Kunther was kinfolk
and a pal.

He took off his clothes,
        grabbed a Trojan rubber and
the tube of K-Y and slipped his dick
        up my ass. Then we began
rocking back and forth. Wow! He
        hit my G-spot again and again.

        After we all came,
we laid together for a
        smile and a "joint" and
enjoyed that post fuck feeling
        of tranquility.

We continue to do this.
        We have become
like a married threesome.
        While we are not formally
married, we feel as one.

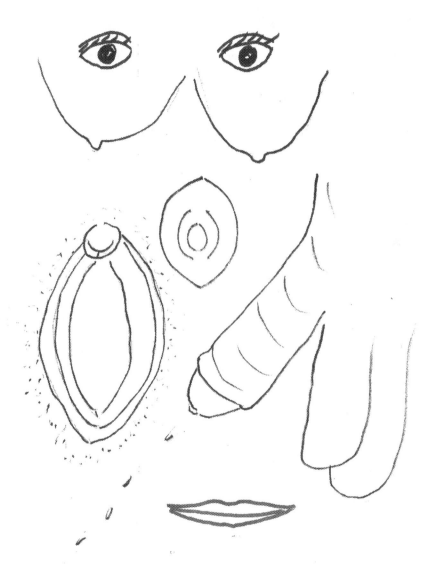

The Power of Love And Lust

Making Love With An Older Guy At The Y.M.C.A.

Went to the Y.M.C.A. to work out
and met a sweaty muscular
        guy named Bill.

Yes, for an older guy
        he had kept himself
in great shape -- what with
        using weights and
the treadmill.

While his hair was gray
        he had it all and
it contrasted nicely
        with his blue eyes.

We looked at each other
        as we used weights and
we both knew we were gay
        and horny for some action.

We left the exercise
        room and
headed for the locker
        room.

As we took off our

shorts and T-shirts,
and jock straps, we had a
        nice chat
about all sorts of things,
        and we smiled,
knowing what each was
        thinking.

We both noticed that
        we were well hung - 8"-.
I was circumcised and he
        was uncut.
But, our testicles were as
        big as lemons.

We took our bubble butts
        down to the
showers before going to
        the spa.

In the all-male spa,
        we laughed and
talked and yes started
        fondling our
cocks and balls.

We did this routine
        for five days
in a row and were
        having a ball.

Then, the 6th day,
        it happened.
Bill looked at me and
        whispered, "Hey
Buddy after we get out,

      we could have some
fun in my van before we
      go home.
So, what about it pal?"

I just smiled and
      nodded my head.
So, off we went
      to his van
that was parked in the
      front lot of the
Y.M.C.A.

When I got to his van,
      I could tell Bill
was well-prepared for action.
      There were curtains
that you could pull to cover
      up the back windows.

So, we got into the back,
      took off our
gym outfits and did some
      cuddling before
some real action.

Wow! I found that sweet
      Bill had thought of
everything. He reached into
      his glove compartment
and got a Trojan and the
      K Y.

I whispered as he put on the
      ribbed rubber,
"Baby, I'm yours; ride me

into ecstasy."

And that he did,
        I got dizzy and
light-headed as I responded
        to his thrusts and
I finally ejaculated.

Cum was all over my chest
        and Bill took his
        tongue and licked it all up.
        And, then he sucked
the head of my cock.
        I yelled with sounds of
total satisfaction.
        I thought, "I've never been
laid like this before."

Afterwards, I took off his
        rubber and
gave him a gentle
        blow job.

Bill and I kept this up
        for weeks.
It made going to the
        Y.M.C.A. something to
look forward to.

At the end of each
        session, I always told
him that for an older guy
        he could really
        FUCK.

He would always

smile and laugh and
say, "Thanks pal. But,
        Buddy, you sure
know how to suck and take
        cock deep.

Yes, we became real buddies.
        Hey, what are true
friends for anyway? A guy knows
        what another guy wants
and needs. What's a friend
        for anyway if not to
meet your physical and emotional
        needs.

        This may seem obscene to some
            but I'm in love with
        the guy. Why? Well, he is kind,
            lovable and tries very
        hard to meet my needs in every way.

        Who knows, maybe some day he
            will look at me and say,
        "Buddy, let's get hitched !"
            And, I will reply,
        "Sure man, you're my super
            STUD."

A Love Affair With A Sexy Ice Hockey Player

I went to a
    hockey game
and fell in love with
    a player named Loretta.

Living and skating with
    Loretta was fantastic.
We would strip and
    skate naked on the
ice after closing.

She would arch her
    bubble butt up
to receive my strong
    9 inch "rocket"
as we skated.

When we went to bed,
    she insisted on
wearing her skates.

Good thing I was circumcised
    because I would have been
after a night sleeping with
    my gorgeous Loretta.

All was going great

        until she complained
that my cock lacked
        the thrust that
she needed to
        reach climax.

She insisted that I
        take a special pill.
I swear it was a steroid.
        She told me it would
give me that extra thrusting
        power that I needed
in my 9 inch "rocket."

Well, that pill worked.
        I found that I got a
heart on that made my dick
        like a "door knob."

For a long time
        after that things
were hot, hot, hot
        between us. My
"door knob" really gave
        her the twist and
thrust that she needed.

                Yes, things were hot between
                us. It's a wonder that
                the ice didn't melt in response
                to our skating with my
                cock up her bubble butt.

                I got an added bonus,
                when I shot out cum,
                I found that I needed

to ejaculate
3 times to completely
feel at peace.

Then, things changed.
In walked a gal named
Betty (nicked named " Butch")
and I was confronted by
a whole different problem.

"Butch" made a play for
Loretta —yes she was
a lesbian and was
attracted to
beautiful athletic gals.

Well, Loretta fell in love
with Betty. Why?
Because she had a better
'door knob" than me.
I sure missed our
midnight skating
sessions — but what
was I to do but
surrender to the lesbian
with a powerful
vibrator that was long, wide
and hard — and
vibrated at 3 speeds.

Buck St.

Welcome To The Pearl Buck Symposium

The Remarkable Pearl Buck -- Session 1

I enjoy reading biographies -- especially about artists and writers. Recently, I happened upon a biography about Pearl Buck written in 1983 by Nora Stirling. At first I hesitated to check it out because I thought I already knew a lot about her. I remembered that she had grown up in China because her parents were serving as Presbyterian missionaries there, that she had written several novels such as **The Good Earth** that are considered classics, that she had won many honors including the Nobel Prize for Literature, and that she had done a great deal to help find homes for interracial children from Asia by establishing Welcome House. But, on an impulse I checked out the biography. Well, I'm very glad that I did because I discovered that I knew very little about Pearl Buck.

Not only did I learn a lot of new things about this famous author, I found that I really liked and admired her as a person. Frankly, after reading biographies on such as writers as Ernest Hemingway, Gertrude Stein, Sinclair Lewis, Dorothy Parker and Truman Capote, I was left with the feeling that while they were very talented, they had a lot of problems. Many were troubled with alcoholism, drug addiction, depression and personality disorders. I definitely felt that it would be difficult to have a long term relationship with them. Not so with Pearl Buck. She was a woman who was not only a talented writer but one who made a significant contribution to humanity. She had problems too but she had the strength from within to deal with them. She became truly a strong, courageous, compassionate person who had herself together. Of course, she was forty before she achieved success. She had by that time experienced poverty, peril, disappointment and heartbreak. All of these things helped her to develop a deeper understanding of human beings and motivated her to achieve a greater good besides enjoying her fame as a writer.

After reading Stirling's biography I was inspired to read other works by or about Pearl Buck. I discovered another more recent biography written by Peter Conn and entitled, **Pearl Buck - A Cultural Biography.** I also reread **The Good Earth** and obtained copies of two of her most famous essays -- "The Child Who Never Grew" and "Essay on Life." I also discovered that she had her critics. Many among the so-called literati felt that by writing too many novels in order to earn money for her humanitarian projects, she had neglected art -- and, it hadn't been worth it. Well, I'll let you be the judge.

In reading about Pearl Buck I was impressed by the fact that she was so bright. She spoke and wrote both Chinese and English. In fact, she first spoke Chinese and then English. It is interesting to note that when she wrote a novel about China she thought of it first in Chinese -- then translated it into English keeping many of the characteristics of the traditional Chinese novel. She was well versed in the classics of Chinese literature. She spent five years translating the long Chinese classic **Shui Hu Chuan** (All Men Are Brothers) which was well received by the critics -- especially in China.

She wrote novels not only about China but India, Korea and Japan. All were well researched. She also wasn't afraid to write essays about civil liberties, racism, women's rights, birth control, religion, foreign policy and education. She had the ability to communicate complex ideas in a meaningful way that appealed to a wide cross section of the reading public. She was especially gifted at verbalizing the emotions and feelings of those caught in difficult situations.

The wellsprings of her writing came from her missionary parents who where both well educated. Her mother encouraged her writing as a child and set an example of showing Christ to the Chinese people not by preaching but by offering them medical help and helping them to meet their basic daily needs. She really tried to set a living example of what a Christian should be. Her father too was an individual committed to a higher calling. However, unlike Pearl Buck's mother all of his energies were spent trying to convert the Chinese through preaching and religious education. From both, Pearl Buck inherited the idea that we are put on this Earth to do good -- and in her case that meant to defend the poor and oppressed. She always strove to enhance social justice for all. She embraced her mother's approach by helping people with their daily concerns and problems. However, she added another element that her mother did not use and that was political action.

Another important source of her writing was the fact that she had personally experienced peril, pain and suffering. She knew what it felt like to be an outsider. The whites in China were the odd ones out with their blue eyes, long noses, blond hair and strange smell. She knew what it was like to feel in mortal danger as a result of the Boxer Rebellion and later in 1926 when the Nationalists and Communists were battling each other over the control of Nanking. It was a miracle that she and her family were not killed on both occasions. Later, she gave birth to a retarded child which in itself caused her to experience the anguish and despair that only those who have been in that situation would be able to relate to.

Welcome Back!

The Pearl Buck Symposium
The Remarkable Pearl Buck -- Session 2

One major challenge Pearl Buck faced before she became famous was dealing with having a retarded child. She had to first accept the fact that Carol, her darling, beautiful little girl was retarded and then try to help her. Indeed, one of the reasons why Pearl Buck began writing fiction was because she needed to earn money to care for Carol. It is interesting to note that she included a retarded child in **The Good Earth.** She pictures the child as being a comfort to her father Wang Lung despite her retardation.

After she began earning a lot of money, she immediately gave a large portion of it for research into mental retardation and for the support of Vinelard Training School for Retarded Children which is located in New England. The Truth about Carol was kept from the public. The entire subject was simply too painful for Pearl Buck to handle publicly. In this endeavor she wrote to friends who knew about Carol and asked them not to give out information about her.

One must remember how people looked at the retarded back in 1930 to appreciate the fears that Pearl had. She herself was still working through the whole painful ordeal. For the next twenty years, Pearl Buck often gave the impression of being standoffish -- especially with reporters. This was largely due to her fear that her "secret" would suddenly be revealed. She was fearful of how the press would handle it and how the public would view her given the ignorance about mental retardation at that time. She especially felt that people lacked empathy with the parents of retarded children.

The secret about Carol wasn't revealed to the public until 1950 when Pearl Buck decided that telling her story would help others in the same situation. She wrote a long article entitled, "The Child Who Never Grew" which was published in the **Ladies Home Journal.** It is beautifully written. In it she describes the feelings that she had as she went through each stage of dealing with the reality of having a mentally handicapped child: recognition that something was wrong, bewilderment at Carol's reactions (for example, when Pearl became upset and cried, Carol would laugh), grief, guilt, anger, dwelling on what might have been, envy of those with normal children, hurt at the way others looked and talked about Carol, acceptance, seeking answers and help, taking the necessary steps for Carol's happiness and then living daily with the solution. The solution in this case was placing Carol in the hands of professionals at Vinelard School. At one point in the article she says that the experience made her become aware that there are two kinds of people in the world -- "those who live with a temporary grief and those who live daily with an on-going, never ending grief."

The publication of the article caused a sensation. In opening the door on herself, she opened the door for thousands of other suffering and grieving parents. Letters poured in from readers in which they described their relief at realizing that they were not alone. By the way she personally answered every letter. Often parents of retarded children would stop by her home unannounced seeking her counsel. She always made it her business to take the time to talk with them. One of the people who read the article was Rose Kennedy who decided to also go public about having a retarded child.

Pearl Buck was a feminist before the word was ever created. So many of her books are about women -- their status in a male dominated society -- their disappointments and heartbreaks. She joined others in strongly advocating birth control, equal opportunities and treatment of women in the work place and the election of women to public office as well as the appointment of women to important agencies. She often appeared on the same platform with such famous women as Eleanor Roosevelt, Margaret Mead, Margaret Sanger and Francis Perkins.

She discovered how difficult it was to be a woman writer in a male dominated publishing world. For example, many of her fellow writers -- all men -- resented the fact that she was awarded the Nobel Prize for Literature. In fact, some were down right nasty about it. Robert Frost of all people remarked, "If she can get it, anybody can." Theordore Dreiser who she thought she knew refused to have anything more to do with her. She also discovered when she wrote books about America rather than China, that they were met with criticism. Often the critics would say, "She really only knows about China." So, she wrote five novels under a pseudonym -- John Sedges. She thought that if she used a man's name in writing about America, that she would find more acceptance. She was right. The critics loved the books.

Her strong feminism originated in her experiences as a child. Her father was an insensitive man who regarded all women as being created to do the bidding of men. He was still alive when **The Good Earth** became an international best seller. Pearl gave him a copy to read. He returned it to her in a week with the comment, "Here take it. I just can't get through it." That was it. Oh, yes, he did wonder about how much money the book would make.

Pearl only received nurturing and encouragement from her mother Carie. Very early she encouraged Pearl to write stories and to try to get them published. Also, she was the one who insisted that Pearl be allowed to go to college. Also, during her upbringing Pearl could see how miserable her mother was with her life as a missionary in far off China and how unhappy she was being married to a man like Absalom Sydenstricker. While she suffered severe bouts of depression, she kept her anger bottled up within her.

Pearl Buck's feminism also came about because of her unhappy first marriage. Her first husband was Lossing Buck who was an agricultural expert working for the Presbyterian mission in China. While he was bright in his chosen field, he did not have the capacity for intimacy. Pearl had hoped for a spouse who would be a true friend and supportive confidant. Well, it simply did not happen. Lossing never did get the message. For example, he did not encourage Pearl's interest in writing. In fact, he felt that she should be happy simply being his secretary and helping him with his career. He controlled the purse strings too. She had to give any money that she earned as a college teacher and later writer to him. When they had Carol, it was Pearl who had to deal with the tough realities of Carol's retardation. Lossing was totally incapable of understanding and supporting his wife in dealing with the situation. Naturally, Pearl felt totally rejected.

Then, she learned that he was having affairs with some of his students at the University of Nanking. That was too much. In response to that she found her own lover -- the famous and handsome Chinese poet Hsu Chih Mo. In her mind she was thinking, "I'm not going to take this like my mother would. No, I have the right to happiness too."

Much later she fell in love with Richard J. Walsh who was her editor for the Day Company. Eventually, both got divorces from the first spouses and were married. Pearl found in Walsh the loving, encouraging friend and confidant that she needed. She always said that she received "freedom as an individual" in her relationship with him. To complete their happiness they adopted six children many of whom were interracial.

After Walsh's death in 1960 she sought the love of another man. This time it was the famous philosopher William Ernest Hocking. He too had recently lost his mate and was looking for love and companionship. Both enjoyed their times together as revealed in their many love letters. The thing to note here is that Pearl Buck believed -- like the true feminist that she was --that as a passionate human being she had the right to seek love to meet her needs. She strongly believed that women were entitled to sexual equality with men. I am sure that some of the women hearing this at this symposium are saying to themselves, "Right on girl!"

Welcome Back!

Symposium on Pearl Buck
The Remarkable Pearl Buck -- Session 3

I found Pearl Buck's personal religious evolution very interesting. Born and raised in a Presbyterian home, she was indoctrinated into the fundamentalist viewpoint and eventually like her parents became a missionary. Then, in light of her own experiences -- especially having to live under two insensitive men -- her father and later her first husband --and having to deal with the reality of a retarded child, she found herself stepping back and reexamining her beliefs. She found that she especially "hated" (that's her word) St. Paul and his views with regard to the position of women in marriage and in the life of the church. Generally, she came to believe that the loving, gentle message of Christ had been perverted by the men who had organized the early Christian church. She eventually separated herself from organized religion and embraced what I would call a combination of humanism and naturalism.

She became totally disenchanted with the missionary movement. In a famous speech at the Astor Hotel in 1932, she discussed why she entertained mixed feelings about her calling as a missionary. She said, "I have seen the missionary narrow, uncharitable, unappreciative, ignorant. I have seen him so filled with arrogance in his own beliefs, so sure that all truth was with him and him only that my heart has knelt with a humbler one before the throne of Buddha rather than before the God of that missionary. I have seen missionaries . . . scornful of any civilization except their own, so harsh in their judgment upon each other, so coarse and insensitive among a sensitive and cultivated people that my heart has fairly bled with shame. I can never have done with my apologies to the

Chinese people that in the name of a gentle Christ we have sent such people to them. . . ignorant ... mediocre . . . arrogant. . . superstitious."

As you can imagine she finished to total silence. Describing the reaction later she wrote: "It was appalling. I felt as if I were alone in the middle of the Sahara. . . . But I sat up straight and looked calm -- I hope. Then clapping began and I had a very great ovation. Evidently there were many people there who agreed with me. . . ." Unfortunately for Pearl the Presbyterian leaders in charge of missions were at first shocked and then angry at her views. She eventually resigned as a missionary because of the controversy caused by her comments. It is interesting to note that she included a missionary in **The Good Earth.** He is a tall, blond man who makes a few remarks to Wang Lung which he doesn't understand and then hands him a picture card showing Jesus on the Cross. When Wang Lung shows the picture to his father, the latter reacts with horror and says, "This man must have done some terrible things to be killed like that." The incident illustrates the wide gap that existed between the ordinary Chinese peasant and the missionary.

After her husband died in 1960, Pearl Buck became intensely interested in the whole topic of immortality. She immediately set out to find some answers. She turned first to scientists -- especially Albert Einstein and Andrew Compton who had helped direct the Manhattan Project. From Compton she received a letter of introduction that she used to meet with other well-known scientists. This involved a lot of travel. She wasn't content to talk with them on the phone or exchange letters with them. No, indeed. Usually, she got in her car and drove to wherever they lived in order to have face-to-face discussions.

Upon rereading Einstein's statement that "Mass is interchangeable with Energy," she experienced what she termed, "an awakening of my mind and the conversion of my soul, the clarification of my spirit, the unification of my whole being." She elaborated, "I had a new concept of death, a new approach to life." Now, in her mind the meaning of eternity became "time without beginning and without end." She understood "that whatever exists now has always existed and always will, the universal and eternal law being only that of change."

From discussions with Andrew Compton she gained his insight into the topic. He felt that science would eventually gain the facts about the relationship between the mass -- the body -- and the mind and the spirit or soul. He told her that "there aren't any miracles only scientific discoveries that solve the mysteries of human existence."

Pearl Buck came to believe along with Compton and others that there is no supernatural but only the supremely natural, the purely scientific. She wrote, "Science and religion, religion and science are two sides of the glass through which one sees darkly until these two, focusing together, reveal truth." She firmly believed that science would some day prove the existence of the soul or spirit (in the form of mass or energy) as separate from the body.

She also turned to her friend and lover William Ernest Hocking for his thoughts. He sent her his book **Meaning of Immortality in Human Experience** and later had many discussions with her about the issue of death and immortality. He reaffirmed in a philosophical way what Einstein and Compton had been saying. He wrote: "The peace that comes to the dying is not of terminus; it is -- as I interpret it -- the peace of handing-on, and of reverting with the felt opening of a perspective more profoundly valid." He told her that he believed that one after death continues the path of complete fulfillment through the actions of an eternally creating and maintaining God (or natural force).

When she was eighty, she wrote an essay entitled "Essay on Life" that was published in **Modern Maturity.** It was one of the most popular articles ever written for that magazine. In the article she discussed her thoughts on immortality. Of course, she drew on the beliefs of Einstein, Compton and Hocking but communicated them in a way all could understand. She wrote: "I have begun to live the eightieth year of my life ....I do not know what people mean when they speak of being old. I do not know because I do not know where life begins, if indeed there is a beginning, and I do not know when it ends, if indeed there is an end. I know that I am in a stage, a phase, a period of life. I entered this life at birth, I shall end this stage with death. For me, death is merely the entrance into further existence. I do not know what that existence will be, but then I did not know what existence in this stage would be when I was born into it. I did not ask to be, but I have been and I am. My reason tells me I shall continue to be. I am on my way somewhere, just as I was on the day of my birth. 'Young' and 'old' for me are meaningless words except as we use them to denote where we are in the process of this stage of being...."

In conclusion, Pearl Buck was certainly not your ordinary novelist. She was a woman who always had a higher purpose in life than simply writing best sellers. She wanted to essentially stand for human rights, the uplifting of the down trotted and rational thinking. When fame came to her, she was uniquely ready for it in the sense of knowing how to build on it and use it in positive ways. She often found herself speaking for those who did not have a voice. By her writing and speaking she made their needs known. The criticism that she neglected art is extremely narrow in its focus. In my opinion she was true to the art of writing -- and true to the art of uplifting and shedding light on human experience. We need more Pearl Bucks today. But, I'll let you be the judge.

Fame St.

The Perils Of Fame

Like the rest of you struggling writers I often find myself dreaming about being discovered and enjoying fame and fortune. I fantasize about being on the cover of **Time** magazine and featured in **The New York Times** under the caption, "B.G. Webb's Novel Is A Timeless Classic."

Well, I've changed my mind about being discovered -- in fact I now live in fear of such a development. Why? Because I have just read about Alf Wight's experiences with being discovered. Alf Wight was the quiet, modest Scottish vet who wrote hugely best selling books under the pseudonym of James Herriot.

The account of Alf Wight's writing career is discussed in a recent biography about him by Graham Lord. I found the account very interesting in terms of filling me in about Wight's background and how he came to become a famous author. Lord elaborates about the cost that Wight paid for becoming the most well known vet in the world. It was that aspect of the book that I found disturbing in terms of my own desire to be suddenly discovered and thrust into the spotlight.

Lord relates how Alf worked very hard to get something published. In fact, he spent ten years submitting stories to magazines and receiving them back without any comment -- good or bad. He was in his early 50s before he published and then his first novel didn't sell very well. It took another novel and some good reviews for him to achieve recognition. After that things really took off -- not only in terms of books but films and a TV series. Eventually, everyone knew about Alf Wight or at least about James Herriot.

Even Alf admitted to Lord and others that he enjoyed the first two years of being in the public's eye. He liked knowing that people were enjoying his books and that he had enough money coming in so that he didn't have to worry about meeting the needs of his family. However, after the first two years, being famous became a burden -- a real chore and a source of worry. It under minded some of the basic happiness and peace of mind that he had had before he became famous. Let me tell you about some of the perils of fame that Alf encountered.

First, despite the fact that Alf had taken pains to create characters that did not resemble people that he knew, several individuals felt sure that he was describing them. Later, many of them especially disliked how these same characters were portrayed in films and TV shows. Even Alf's wife disliked how certain actresses would play Herriot's wife because she felt that they were really portraying her. Unfortunately, Alf had a hard time taking the heat about how his characters resembled some of the people in his life. In order to avoid disputes and especially libel suits, he paid them off. The one who got the most money was his partner who believed that he was the Siegfried -- Herriot's partner in the novels.

Second, another problem developed as a result of many interviews that he had with reporters. They wanted all sorts of detailed information about his life -- his parents, schooling, military service during World War II, marriage and children. Well, Alf found it difficult to be entirely up front about everything. According to Lord, Alf's responses to many questions reflected his reactions to his upbringing in a very class conscious English society. He felt inferior because of his humble beginnings. He tended to hide things (such as the true occupations of his father and mother) and feel subservient to his so-called "betters."

Third, another problem was that the real Alf became lost. The public expected Alf to be James Herriot. And, in strange twist Alf did not want to disappoint his public. So, he tried to become what they expected. But, after awhile he found it more and more difficult to deal with the situation. The real Alf was different in so many ways from the fictional James Herriot. Alf began to feel that he was living a double life.

Fourth, he had to deal with the temptation of allowing the big money that he was now making change the life that had made him happy. He was basically content to be a country vet in Yorkshire. He resisted changing too much. He continued to live a very simple down to earth existence.

Fifth, another problem that was related to having so much money was the temptation to move elsewhere to avoid paying the high income taxes.

For years he had to pay 85% of what he made -- later the tax was reduced to 50%. He and his wife explored several other places to live (Switzerland and Spain) and finally decided that they would gladly give the government what it wanted because they loved living in Yorkshire.

By the way Alf often told close friends that he was happy that he was old when fame and fortune came knocking because he was able to resist changes that would have under minded his happiness. He knew what made him happy and he wanted to maintain those things in his life.

Sixth, some of the citizens of his hometown of Thirsk believed that Alf wasn't doing enough for the town. Of course, Alf disagreed with his hometown critics. He felt that he had attracted a lot of tourists who spent a lot of money at local businesses. Also, he urged his fans to contribute to the local animal shelter.

Seventh, some of the citizens of the town felt that Alf's fame had ruined the town and the surrounding quiet and beautiful area. According to them, he had caused the town to become another tourist trap -- another Disneyland -- another Strafford upon Avon. And, to be fair, things had changed a lot in quiet Thirsk. During the summer 50 to 60 fans would show up everyday at the so-called "surgery" to see James Herriot -- or should I say Alf Wight -- and in some cases they had brought their dogs and cats for him to treat.

Also, you had the other trappings of a tourist trap: the Herriot Trail; the Herriot restaurant; Herriot calendars, guidebooks, writing paper; the Herriot Gift Shop (where you could buy photos of the stars that appeared in the films and TV series and miniature statues of Herriot and many of the animals that he treated); the Herriot Tea Shop (where one could buy some Herriot marmalade); and finally the Herriot Pub where you could buy Herriot's favorite beer and sandwich.

Of course, Alf pointed out that he didn't start any of these things. Local entrepreneurs were responsible for all of these mindless but lucrative enterprises. Well, not everyone was willing to see it his way. In their minds Alf Wight's novels had started all the negative changes in the town and the surrounding countryside.

Finally, writing for Alf instead of being a pleasure became a chore. He experienced burn out. He grew weary of taking pains with his work. He ran out of ideas. He turned down all sorts of requests for plays, scripts for

TV shows, stories for magazines because he was simply exhausted by the whole business of being famous.

James Herriot had became a real burden. For example, bundles of fan mail -- sometimes as many as 50 to 100 letters -- would come each day for James Herriot. Alf spent much of each day answering his fan mail and also signing photographs of himself to include in his responses. Well, after years of this, he started becoming unglued.

His experience reminds me of how Sir Arthur Conan Doyle came to regard his creation of the character of Sherlock Holmes. The public clamored for more and more stories about the famous detective. It never seemed to be satisfied. The whole business of Holmes became a burden -- a source of anxiety -- to Doyle. Well, that's how Alf felt too -- but about James Herriot.

During all of this time one must give Alf credit for maintaining a calm, warm and friendly outward manner despite how he felt inside. He would greet his fans cheerfully, sign photographs, and take a look at their pets. He answered many requests for public appearances and interviews. He travelled

Death St.

Grief And Relief

You have just gone thru the ultimate tragedy.
You have seen the great love of your life to the end.

First you realized that something was very wrong,
Then came the endless medical parade,
The doctors, the hospital, the tests and more tests,
The treatments tried and the treatments abandoned,
The hopes raised and the hopes dashed,
Then the inevitable pronouncement,
"We can do no more."

All the weight of the family fell on you.
You managed all, his part and yours too.
You cared for him as you could, and
Then arranged for more care.
You supported him and he died.

The grief and relief both came.
The relief does not lesson the grief,
And the grief does not condemn the relief.
Let them both fill your very soul.
Only then can you heal,
Heal and rebuild.
There is life left for you.

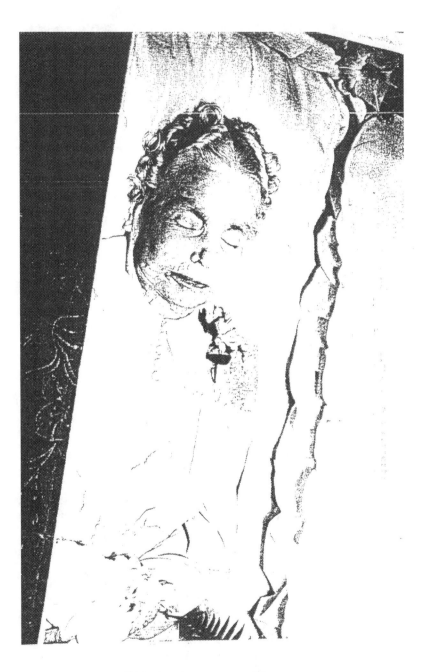

Off To My Next Form of Existence

Learning To Walk Alone

We got our signals crossed, Lorraine did not go with me.
I went alone to the Garden.
Yes it was better to go alone for the first time
But I was so alone!

Before, I would occasionally like to go somewhere alone.
A sense of freedom went with being by myself.
Then I was alone by choice;
Now I am just alone.

I watched the other walkers as I had never watched them before,
Family groups, young couples, pairs of women and old couples,
Oh the stab of jealousy when I see an old couple.
But no men without woman or child.

As I neared the Japanese Garden I saw another lone woman
She looked as miserable as I felt. Was she crying too?
Then as I neared the pool by the Climatron,
Another lone woman, and she smiled at me!

It was a cold wintry day; nothing would be in bloom.
The winter aconite? No, the Woodland Garden is blocked off
But wait, there they are, the spring Witch Hazel is in bloom!
Spring will come!

I will not try to avoid places we enjoyed together
No need to learn to be alone. I am alone.
Friends can often fill the empty feeling,
But I must learn to walk alone.

Walking Alone

Blind St.

The following pieces were written by my late wife LOUISE WEBB.

Surrounded by Fog in a Sighted World

I feel as if I am walking around - literally - in a fog. I hear voices, but I don't know where they are coming from. I see shadowy figures, but I don't know who they are.

Diabetes is an insidious affliction. It is robbing me of my eyesight. I have a wrinkled retina in one eye and cataracts on both eyes, but the doctors refuse to remove cataracts because of the risks due to diabetes. Nothing can be done about the retina.

I have sought second and third opinions. Stronger lenses in my glasses would not help because of the cataracts. Doctors tell me the only thing I can do is keep my blood sugar under tight control with lots of exercise and a strict diet. No wonder I sometimes get depressed.

Diabetics must test their blood often. I have trouble seeing the drop of blood and the small area where it goes on the test strip.

Being diabetic means a rigid lifestyle. There is little room for spontaneity, especially for one who hates schedules.

There are stages of grief: disbelief, denial, anger, self-pity, coming to terms, acceptance and learning to cope. I am going through these stages because I have a loss - my sight. It's like losing an old friend.

Right now I am in the anger stage. I ask, "Why me? I didn't ask for this."

As if don't have enough problems, I must deal with the reactions of others. I've noticed that if one is sick, people tend to run in the other direction, for fear of being asked to do something. When one loses his/ her sight, people run away faster and farther. They probably fear the unknown and don't know what they can do for me. I guess they are reminded of their own mortality.

The loss of sight brings about other losses. I can no longer drive a car, use a computer, do a jigsaw puzzle, go to a store by myself, read a newspaper, read music, hold a job, prepare a meal or do needlework or crafts. I have totally lost my independence.

I am like a six-year-old. I can dress, feed and bathe myself; but I can't prepare the food, see the colors of clothes or apply my makeup.

When I go out, I have to be accompanied by a sighted person, who 99.99% of the time is my husband, Bud. I have a white cane to help me with steps and curbs.

I cannot see facial features clearly. I need to be six inches away from a person to see him or her. I rely on voice recognition. God only knows how many acquaintances think I have snubbed them.

I try not to focus on what I cannot do, but what I can do. I am trying to adjust and become more independent within my foggy world.

I have magnifiers in every room and in the car. My easy chair is as close to the TV as possible. I eat from a dark-colored plate because most of what I eat is light in color.

I have a calculator and telephone with large keys. I memorize the number of steps from one place to another, as well as the location of keys on the TV remote, microwave and telephone. I put my many pills on a white paper towel so I can see them.

I sought help from the St. Louis Society for the Blind. They have support groups where I have met others in my same situation. I learned the fundamentals of braille.

The Wolfner Library in Jefferson City, a subsidiary of the Library of Congress, provides books on tape, postage free. These tapes are a real Godsend. They help pass many lonely hours. I have "read" about 120 books in the last year and a half.

I must say the world could make itself more "blind - friendly." At the Art Museum, for example, the guards are constantly reminding me to "step behind the line." I simply moved closer to read the tiny plaque beside the painting.

There should be a law that all lettering - print and on TV - should be in black on a white background. And it should be in LARGE LETTERS! Fancy script should be outlawed.

I am slowly learning to live in my foggy world. I rely more on hearing, touch, taste and smell. I am reviving interests I had before the fog sidetracked me, such as writing.

I have not lost the ability to think and to string two or more sentences together. I keep reminding myself that the great poet John Milton was able to compose Paradise Lost when he was blind by dictating it to his daughters. Bud is my secretary/transcriber, another of his many duties as my caregiver.

I feel I am making progress. It is a learning experience. As Eleanor Roosevelt said, "We learn from living and experiencing both the good and the bad."

Aladdin Comes To Stay

Bud, Crystal and I have a new apartment mate. He is a good companion. He doesn't eat anything; he doesn't make messes or play loud music. He never complains or gets angry. All he requires is an electrical outlet to plug into and a corner of my desk. His manufacturer named him Aladdin Classic, which he proudly wears like a name tag beneath his video screen. We just call him Aladdin. He is my new video magnifier.

The year 2002 was a year of loss for me. I had to give up reading printed material, driving, sewing, needlework and crafts, playing the piano and cooking, to name just a few of my losses. I felt that I had completely lost my independence. By Christmas, I was about ready to throw in the towel, along with the pills, the insulin shots, the diet and the exercise. I had enjoyed reading all my life until cruel old Mother Nature took it away.

Instead, I decided to take some positive action and get a video magnifier. I went to the Society for the Blind and shopped for one. I chose the simplest one, which turned out to be the least expensive, as well as the most popular.

Linda at the Society gave me the name of the salesman. I called him and he said that he just happened to have my choice in stock and would bring it out to me the next day.

When Pat, the salesman, came in the door carrying Aladdin, I knew that things would be different from now on.

Aladdin is 22 inches tall, with a width of 15.6 inches and a depth of 21.5 inches. He weighs 37 lbs. His black and white video screen measures 14 inches diagonally. He magnifies up to 35 times. His video screen is 7 inches above his moveable tray, which can slide forward and backward as well as from side to side.

He has only four controls. An on-off switch along with a knob for focus are on his front. On his left side there is a sliding lever which changes the background from white with black print to black with white print with shadings between black and white. Finally, on his right side is a sliding lever which controls the degree of magnification that I require.

Pat showed me the controls and I started reading everything that I could get my hands on -- the dictionary, the phone book, letters, bills and a cookbook. I even threaded a needle! I still have to get used to seeing my huge fingers.

Then I learned to write with Aladdin. This gets tricky because I have to watch the screen at the same time that my pen is on the paper. It requires good hand - eye coordination. Pat suggested using paper with heavy lines to keep me from writing all over the place. It was great holding a normal size pen in my hand.

Aladdin costs $1,800. Thank goodness I was willing to settle for a black -and- white model. Color models run about $3,000. Medicare and most insurance companies will not cover the cost. However, I am trying to get my insurance company to pay for all or part of it.

Bud and I could have taken a nice trip for the cost of Aladdin. But how much scenery can a half-blind person see? I would rather be able to function better around the house.

As you know, Aladdin in literature had a magic lamp. My Aladdin is my magic lamp, making my dim world a lot brighter.

I feel that I have regained some of my lost independence. And I can now fill out our income tax returns, which thrills me no end (ha ha).

By the way, I am reading this from the pages you are holding in your hands. But what I see is several times larger.

Louise could play by ear. But, she needed to
see the notes of the start of the song

(Score of Memory)

She printed in large letters the opening notes so she
could play for various Masonic groups.

Every Street lamp
   seems to bear
A fatalistic warning
Someone mutters + a street
   lamp gutters
Soon it will be morning.
Daylight, I must wait for the
   sunrise
I must think of a new life
And I mustn't give in
When the dawn comes tonight
   there'll be a memory too
And a new day will begin.
Burnt out ends of smoky days
The stale cold smell of morning
the street lamp dies
Another night is over Another day is dawning

Private St.

Private Journeys

I think that part of being human is the need to make private journeys to places that have special meaning for us. They are journeys that we usually make by ourselves or with someone we trust. Here are some examples of what I'm talking about.

Recently, I have been reading about veterans of World War II returning to the battlegrounds of that great war. I remember one vet who had been part of the D-Day invasion of Normandy. He felt compelled to return to the very beach where he landed. He looked at the terrain, visited the nearby cemetery, looked at all the crosses and eventually fell to his knees and cried.

I remember reading about Eleanor Roosevelt taking her friend Lorena Hickok to see the beautifully carved figure "Grief" marking the grave of the wife of Henry Adams. She had committed suicide after learning that her husband was having an affair. Eleanor told Lorena that she often visited the grave after learning about her husband's love affair with Lucy Mercer. She told her friend that she always felt better and stronger by visiting the statue. For her it represented a woman who had transcended pain and hurt to achieve serenity.

Of course, while Eleanor was undertaking her private journeys, Franklin Roosevelt was too. He loved to leave the White House and return to Hyde Park to stay at Springwood and to drive his car through the estate pass spots that meant so much to him. He seemed to gain so much comfort and renewed energy from simply visiting places that reminded him of his boyhood days growing up along the Hudson River.

As a child I learned that people go on these private journeys by an incident that occurred when I was ten-years-old. I was playing in the backyard when a woman who must have been in her 60s appeared. She asked if she could come into the yard for a few minutes. Since she seemed to be a very friendly and sincere person, I said, "Yes." Well, she came into the yard and scrutinized every part of it. Then, she turned to me and told me why she had wanted to see it. She explained, "I was married here 50th years ago on this very day. My parents lived in your house then and decided to have my wedding in the garden. My husband has been dead for over twelve years but something made me want to come back to this place. We had such a wonderful life together -- and this is where it all started. Of course, the house and the garden are different but I can still imagine the wedding being here. Thanks for letting me see it."

The first time that I ever took such a journey was in 1947. I had just started 7th grade at John Deere Junior High School. I felt overwhelmed by the large building, different teachers, trying to unlock my hall locker and meeting so many new kids. I remember wanting to go back to my old grade school and be in 6th grade again. So, in a way I did go back. When Willard had its school fair in early October, I found myself leaving the first floor where the activities were being held and climbing the familiar wooden staircase to the second floor. Once I got there, I went into my old classroom by way of the cloakroom. I went over to the desk that I used to have and sat down. I sat there in the semi-darkness for a long time looking around at the bulletin boards and the familiar cozy room. It was the first time that I experienced the idea that I was going from one life experience to another -- and that things could change radically.

Why do humans seem to need to go back? What do these journeys provide us that make us want to undertake one journey after another during our life times. Here are some of my thoughts about the question.

I think that for many of us there is an innate need to go back to certain spots where something important happened to us. In some cases the journey may involve the return to the site of a major life change -- a wedding, a graduation, the birth of a child, a loss of someone dear. It could be a place that brought us happiness or sadness. But, the important thing to note is that we seem to need to go back to see the actual site and visualize the happening. Often, in my case, I find that I am going back to familiar places where I recall common, everyday sorts of things. But, now they seem very important to me. I recently made a trip back to see the house in which I grew up. The memory that gave me the most comfort was remembering everyone being home for lunch and sharing what was going on in our lives that day. That kind of memory is what Thornton Wilder was talking about in his play Our Town. As you recall his theme in that work was that it is important for us to appreciate the everyday sorts of things and relationships -- really stop and look around us and especially appreciate the people in our lives.

There seems to be a need to go to certain places in order to feel closer to someone we loved -- someone with whom we shared an important moment. Perhaps, just by going back to a specific spot we feel their presence. Often widows and widowers feel the need to go back to the church or temple in which they were married or to return to the place where they first met their future husband or wife or where they first fell in love.

Perhaps some of us want to go back to a particular place where we were very happy. The trip may be undertaken at a time when our present life is filled with turmoil. The trip helps us to realize that there are many ups and downs to life and that we can be happy again. Returning to our special happy place gives us comfort. Of course, in some cases it may be an attempt by the person to go home again. And, as we remember Thomas Wolf's warning in You Can't Go Home Again, it is foolish to try. Well, it may be impossible to do so, but I'm sure we all try to do it once in a while. While it may not be the answer to all our problems, at least it gives us some temporary escape and comfort.

In some cases people return to certain spots to confront their fears. The places are connected with pain and suffering for them but they feel they must return to confront the demons of the past and in so doing rid themselves of the nightmares and ghosts that haunt them. I have heard that many survivors of battles, natural disasters and man- made ones have this need. The whole experience can be very therapeutic.

Another thought is that such journeys represent a life-long search for meaning -- meaning to our lives and to life in general. In going back we are reviewing our lives -- seeing where we have been and where we are going. As we go back we review in our minds what life lessons we have learned -- both from the bad and good experiences. The review process helps us understand ourselves better and others too. It gives us perspective. Perhaps, we learn to forgive others and ourselves -- to be thankful for the good things that have happened to us -- and accepting of the lessons we have had to learn from the bad times. Actually going back to the site may cause us to see things differently -- discover some aspect of the happening that we had forgotten or not fully realized before.

Taking private journeys may also be used to show someone that we really trust them with our innermost thoughts. I believe when we take someone with us to see our special place, we are doing it to help that person understand us better. We believe that showing the person the actual place will help them understand what happened to us -- will make what we have to tell them -- what we want to reveal about ourselves -- more believable. That's what Eleanor was telling Lorena.

Some of us make private journeys in order to prepare ourselves for some challenge -- some crisis or perhaps the next stage that we have decided to undertake in our lives. We seem to look into the past for certain places that gave us confidence -- that remind us of our evolution as a person -- of other challenges and changes that we faced and handled successfully. FDR's trips to Springwood and Warm Springs, Georgia did that for him.

Often the need to go on private journeys takes place in our 40s when many of us become interested in family history. We come across some reference to an old family burial plot or a homestead or a country town connected with our family. Suddenly, we have a strong compulsion to go to the cemetery, the homestead, the town. In going on these private trips we are trying to understand our family better -- and in so doing understand ourselves too -- how we fit into the whole scheme of things.

In my opinion another reason we may take private journeys is that it is part of the process involved in preparing for death. Years ago I remember reading a story in my home town's newspaper about the discovery of an unidentified body on the banks of the Mississippi River. There was even a sketch of the middle aged man included in the story with the hope that someone would recognize him. The thing that was unusual about the case was that the man was nicely dressed and groomed. He was found still wearing his glasses. Apparently someone had taken his watch, wedding ring and wallet. He apparently had died of a heart attack because no wounds were found on the body. Much later a woman from Chicago came forward and identified the body as that of her father's. She told authorities that while he had lived most of his life in the Chicago area, he had been born and raised in the Quad Cities. Could it be that he was making a private trip back to a site of a happy childhood memory? I think so.

In conclusion, if you have a strong desire to undertake a private journey to some special spot, by all means go. It is a very innate and natural part of human nature. Indeed, such trips are essential to human beings -- they not only enrich our lives by giving us greater insight into ourselves and the human condition but they provide healing and renewal for our spirits -- our very souls.

Insight St.

Night of the Black Moon in Winter

Snowflakes

It was snowing and I just had to go walking, walking in the snow. How neat!

> Besides, the birds had arrived at the bird feeder and it needed to be refilled.
>
> The huge white snowflakes floated down to the pavement And then they disappeared.
>
> One moment they were the very essence of fragile beauty,
>
> And then in a split-second they were gone.
>
> They no longer existed; they were completely gone.
>
> The thought came: so it will be with me.

Again as I crossed the yard to the bird feeder, my mind played with the falling flakes.

Like us, they came in all sizes; not all were big and beautiful, but like us all were unique, each in his own pattern.

Some seemed too much in a hurry to float; they came straight down Some were tossed by the wind and rushed to and fro in a great hurry to get somewhere, anywhere!

And then there were the big beautiful pieces of art. But if they fell on the dark pavement, they disappeared; they were no more.

Only those that fell on other snowflakes survived, but were lost in the crowd.

The unique arrangements of the molecules shifted as they compacted. Individually the snowflakes no longer existed.

They either melted or became a part of the snow bank and eventually just part of the huge ice sheet, glacier or iceberg.

No matter what, the beauty of the snowflake no longer existed. So be it with us.

Those of us who just must go it alone on the bare pavement,
disappear.

Man, woman or child can only really exist as the mind interacts
with others.

And those who go with the flow, merge with the crowd
and are gone forever.

Like the snowflake their individuality is compromised.

Is there are middle ground?

Can I be just me and still be part of the whole?

Backyard Temple

I sometimes struggle with the fact that I don't like to go to any temple or church for regular religious services. Yet, I do have my own spiritual place that serves me very well. Two of the walls are consist of bushes and trees while the other two walls consist of the back of the house and the doors to the shed. The ceiling is the blue sky above; the floor is the gravel on the patio and the green back lawn. The furniture is white plastic with a table on which to put my four to five "prayer" books---really various meditation books by writers that touch my soul. I can shift the chairs to prop up my feet, or I can move them to stay in the morning shade. My prayers stay in my head and heart or are "spoken" into my purple spiral notebook. The temperature is controlled by Nature, not by a thermostat; today, it is warm with a gentle comforting breeze. I'm not lacking beautiful artistic inputs––the choir of birds provide their lovely songs; the red hibiscus flowers are as glorious a reminder of God's glory as is the eternal light above the ark. True, there's no community with me at this moment to share in this prayerful time. But somehow I know in other spots all over the world, there are others taking in the glory of Nature and finding, just as I am, gifts that lift them above the usual human experience to whatever is their own sense of spirituality and/or God.

Lifting the veil to see the truth

Concluding Thoughts About Your Journey Down The Lamp Lighted Streets

Well, did you gain any new insight from the lamplights that lit your path as you journed down the streets? I hope you did.

SOUNDS OF A MANTRA FROM THE GURU
"OM OM OM"

In my opinion in order to have a true understanding of the world around us one must be willing to hear all sides, view all sides and have a wide variety of experiences and most important be willing to go bravely into the unknown.

SOUNDS OF A MANTRA FROM THE GURU
"OM OM OM"

It certainly makes life more exciting -- makes one's journey through life more of an adventure. It certainly helps the traveler understand things much better. He or she does not experience the journey of life in darkness but in the light or at least in the moonlight.

SOUNDS OF A MANTRA FROM THE GURU
"OM OM OM"

As your guru I hope you have learned the following in your psychedelic trip:

Listen to the doubters and those who question because they open up doors to different perspectives that help solve the mysteries of life.

The forces that created our universe are far more complex than most of us understand. Read something by Stephen Hawking if you don't believe me.

Religions emerged as part of our evolution as a species so that could we could survive.

The world around us often seems surreal --bizarre--because of the conflicting aspects of human nature and various cultures. The nature of the conflicts remain the same; only the cast of characters have changed.

Civilization as we call it is still in a very primitive and savage stage and at any time (given the right factors) may revert backward to an even more savage stage. It has happened before in the history of mankind.

Human beings are difficult to understand or predict (in terms of behavior) because of their DNA and what Freud and Jung referred to as the Ego, ID and Superego .

Sexual energy is a very powerful aspect of humans as a species and can result in behaviors that various cultures call "good" and "bad."

Humans as a species can be very creative and innovating in terms of art, literature, music and survival and dealing with adversity.

Each human seems to need places to hide. Often they do so by creating a persona for public view. Most need to make private journeys to recharge their energies and emotions.

Our ability to dream, wish and fantasize evolved in order for us to cope with the harsh realities of life. They give us comfort and joy. They also allow people to vent their anger and fears in less harmful ways.

The death experience is one of the most difficult one for humans to accept and understand. The loss of a loved one is met in different ways. Find comfort in the fact that in the natural world all things are recycled. Since humans are part of that natural world, our bodies and spirits (soul, personality, id) will continue to exist in some form.

One doesn't need to have all the answers about the universe to be happy and content. Happiness comes from feeling you are doing something that will make a positive contribution to the species.

Remember to always look to the ways of NATURE to understand human behavior and the universe.

Guru:

"Go on your journey through life with my blessings."

SOUNDS OF INDIAN MUSIC

SOUNDS OF A MANTRA FROM THE GURU

"OM OM OM"

'84

About The Author

B.G. Webb was born in Germany and was brought to this country after the Night of the Broken Glass in 1938.

He grew up in Moline, Illinois and earned a B.A. from Augustana College and a M.A. in history from the University of Illinois.

He taught social studies for thirty-three years, mainly at Webster Groves High School in St. Louis County.

In retirement he became interested in creative writing.

He has published the following books: Echoes and Shadows of Life, Nights of the Black Moon and Days of Sunshine, Dreams, Wishes and Fantasies of Common Folk and Home Front Diary––1944––A Family's Awakening to Truth and Courage.

In retirement he also became a stand-up comic in some of the "joints" and "dives" in the greater St. Louis area. His stage name was Buddy Alley. Under that pen name Author House published his book Zany Humor for Elves, Imps and Clowns.

Xlibris published another humorous book that he wrote entitled "Dear Penis, My Love!": A Hilarious Study of a Penis Obsession under the pen name of Louise Webb. In it he writes funny take offs of the classics–– everything from plays by Shakespeare to poems by Chaucer.

In 2017 Author House published his humorous book entitled, Jolly Humor To Tickle Your Funny Bone.